"*Anxious about Decisions: Finding* is packed with biblical wisdom that is profoundly comforting, gentle, and practical. Michael Gembola astutely addresses the many reasons we struggle with making decisions. After reading it, you will understand how to navigate decisions with humble confidence, knowing that Jesus holds you amid your fears and uncertainties."

Darby Strickland, Faculty and counselor, Christian Counseling & Educational Foundation (CCEF); author of *Is it Abuse?*

"Michael Gembola's book, *Anxious about Decisions*, is one of the most helpful books I have ever read, being clearly written and supremely relevant. Which one of us has not fretted over pending decisions? Gembola cites Scripture frequently and draws on an impressively wide array of Christian thinkers, ending each chapter with practical questions for reflection, making this book perfect for individual or group study. I cannot wait to make it available to my parishioners!"

Christopher A. Hutchinson, Senior Pastor, Grace Covenant Presbyterian Church, Blacksburg, VA; author of *Rediscovering Humility*

"Remarkable. Michael helpfully identifies the new variants of today's anxieties and then he gathers the insights of wise people and joins them with his own pastoral wisdom in a way that actually gives direction."

Edward T. Welch, Faculty and counselor, Christian Counseling & Educational Foundation (CCEF); author of *A Small Book for the Anxious Heart*

"I could not help but think of several people in my life who would immediately benefit from Michael Gembola's latest offering—*Anxious about Decisions*. Well-written, well-researched, and brimming with wise and biblical insight, this book brings both a skill and a humanity to an often-overlooked issue. Those who find themselves anxious and in need of help will find Michael a patient and understanding guide, helping you toward a deeper faith in Christ."

Jonathan D. Holmes, Executive Director, Fieldstone Counseling; coauthor of *Rescue Skills*

"Drawing upon years of experience in counseling those who are anxious about both big and small decisions, Michael Gembola thoughtfully and winsomely leads readers to deeper insights about their anxiety and provides Christ-centered, practical suggestions for facing their fears and finding freedom from decision paralysis and endless rumination. Debating whether you should read this book or not? Gembola would say that you have freedom before God to choose either option. (But if you take the risk and buy it, I'm 99.9% sure you won't regret it!)"

Michael R. Emlet, Dean of Faculty and Counselor, Christian Counseling & Educational Foundation (CCEF); author of *Saints, Sufferers, and Sinners*

"Decision anxiety is real, but so is the peace that God offers. The pages of this book are packed with practical and biblical ways to process your anxiety. It will help you get to what is at the core of your decision anxiety and point you to the peace of God."

Eliza Huie, Licensed and biblical counselor; director of counseling, McLean Bible Church, Vienna, VA; coauthor of *The Whole Life*

ANXIOUS ABOUT DECISIONS

FINDING FREEDOM IN THE PEACE OF GOD

Michael Gembola

New Growth Press

newgrowthpress.com

New Growth Press, Greensboro, NC 27401
newgrowthpress.com
Copyright © 2022 by Michael Gembola

Cover Design: Studio Gearbox, studiogearbox.com
Interior Design and Typesetting: Gretchen Logterman

ISBN: 978-1-64507-256-0 (Print)
ISBN: 978-1-64507-257-7 (eBook)

Library of Congress Cataloging-in-Publication Data on file

Printed in the United States of America

29 28 27 26 25 24 23 22   1 2 3 4 5

For Mom

CONTENTS

INTRODUCTION

"Come to me, all you who are weary and burdened,
and I will give you rest." — Matthew 11:28

The basic message I want you to take away from this book is that God uses your decision-making to help you grow up and mature as a Christian. Decision-making is an arena for spiritual formation. This arena especially has the potential to bring you toward a greater sense of peace, steadiness, and confidence in living out your calling. Living from a sense of calling can feel complicated if you experience significant or extreme decision anxiety and if you suffer from intrusive and obsessive thoughts. Those more profound struggles can be particularly crippling, so they are part of the focus of this book, but much of what I'll say will still be applicable to those who experience the less severe irritations and pains of feeling periodically stuck in times of decision.

Decision anxiety covers a set of feelings and behaviors that interrupt, complicate, or excessively slow down our decisions. It includes feelings of fear, panic, or a lasting unsettledness that is excessive or doesn't fit the circumstances.

For most of us, some degree of anxiety complicates our decision-making and our sense of calling as Christians. We often just don't know what to do, and we wonder what God wants us to do. What is our calling? We hear this in Micah 6:8.

> He has shown you, O mortal, what is good.
>   And what does the Lord require of you?
> To act justly and to love mercy
>   and to walk humbly with your God.

Everyday decisions are opportunities to apply this broad call personally. In our life decisions, such as whether to remain as a high school teacher or go back to school for nursing, we will be more spiritually grounded when we think about pursuing options that provide a way for us to live out our calling, but often the specific answer will not be clear or obvious on this front. Most professions provide daily opportunities to be just, merciful, and humbly walking with God. Making good decisions is about growing in wisdom and skill to apply the principles of the broad Christian calling to the specifics of our lives, in humble dependence on God and in community with wise helpers.

Outside of what's covered in the Ten Commandments and the golden rule, decisions are usually not about discovering God's will in the specifics, because God doesn't typically tell us what decisions to make, and he doesn't hide from us the things he wants us to know. For example, we know a lot more about *how* he wants us to live than where he wants us to live, what he wants us to do for work once we get there, and who to pursue this calling with. There's more to God's will than we know, and we never uncover all the mysteries. God is kind to give us what he wants us to know, but it's humbling to consider how much remains unknown to us (Deuteronomy 29:29; 1 Corinthians 2:9–12; 2 Peter 1:3).

To be a creation rather than the Creator means our knowledge is partial, incomplete, and limited. There's no way around the unknowns that drive decision anxiety. That may sound disappointing, but please don't stop reading here. God has big plans for our big decisions, and he has something to offer us for the small ones too. Although in one sense anxiety or worry is something we do, we also typically experience indecisiveness as an affliction, something that happens to us or in us that hurts. And God has much to say to suffering people.

God has often led his people through times of wilderness, through valleys where death casts a long shadow, and through times of suffering when his strength is made perfect in our weakness. Uncertainty, danger, and risk are forms of suffering that are never pleasant. But he offers us something better than certainty and the absence of risk: he promises to be with us. And when the Good Shepherd is leading us, we find that he uses our times of decision-making to form us in two ways: he makes us more peaceful and makes us better stewards. The longer and closer we walk with the Good Shepherd, the more the decisions coming from our hearts are aligned with his heart.

PEACE

When we give up trying to uncover God's plan in all the details, it opens the door to look for something else. We can start seeking his peace, a spiritual steadiness right in the middle of the uncertainty—this is the kind of peace that passes understanding (Philippians 4:7). We start looking for rest, calm, and trust that we experience in our relationship with God. And so we walk with this little light of mine, a lamp for our feet shining on a few steps of the path. We accept the uncertainty, take a deep breath, and as Emily P. Freeman (and also Princess Anna in *Frozen II*) says, do "the next right thing."[1] To embrace peace is not to strive for certainty in our decisions, and to some extent, not to wait for God to intervene and make our decisions for us. We make decisions best when we understand

God has given us his presence, peace, and guidance in his Word and among his people, and that at the end of the day, we ourselves are invited to make decisions.

I wonder if this sounds unspiritual. Doesn't God's Spirit lead us in decision-making? Some people speak about frequently feeling a sense of God's leading, and they talk about getting nudges and clarity when they fast and pray. Sometimes the stories are compelling—for example, feeling the sudden urge to call someone, only to discover a chance to meet an urgent need. I've certainly felt things like this, and I've often wished this would happen more frequently. I've at times wished God would step in and make certain decisions so that I wouldn't have to; I've wanted him to convey the right answer to me through other people or through strong and clear feelings. Some believers might encourage me to give more time to really listen for God in this way and to give more space to weigh my feelings as a venue of God's possible leading. Although I don't quite share their perspective, I want to leave space for the kind of humility that listens to their encouragement because Christians certainly believe in a God who cares about the details of our lives and inter-venes for good. We'll consider this more in chapter 3.

Regardless of our desire for impressions from God, believers who struggle with anxiety rarely experience moments of clear, felt leading from God. And even if we did, our most spiritual impulses still need to be shaped by biblical wisdom and humility in community. My own conviction is that God is more interested in growing us up as Christians and helping us learn how to make wise decisions, rather than making decisions for us via impres-sions or authority figures. To think that our decisions are to some extent up to us can be a scary thought. But it's only scary if we're alone in those decisions and if the ultimate outcome for our bodies and souls is up to chance or totally dependent on our own wisdom. God can use even our mistakes and failures for our good and his glory. Personal decision-making isn't isolated independence but connected maturity and agency. We're free to do, free to act, and especially free to love God and neighbor. This is the free, mature, active life God has for us. And in all of our decision-making, the Holy Spirit never leaves or forsakes us. God is kind to give us his Spirit, who leads us toward what matters most, but it is in God's time and in God's ways. And in the last day, he will unveil his mysterious working—we will see how he has worked greater good out of our small good, and how he has subverted or overturned all the bad done to us or by us (Romans 8:28).

My general sense is that believers who struggle with decision anxiety aren't helped by giving more time and attention to possible impressions from the Spirit. Instead, the focus of our prayer and reflection should be on the kinds of things the Spirit promises in the Bible, especially his promise to bring us to peace. Peace is a fruit of the Spirit (Galatians 5:22)—God grows peacefulness in us as both an experience and as a way of life. Peace is part of what it means to be wise (James 3:17–18). Peace, in the sense of not being tossed around and constantly shaken, is also part of Christian maturity. To be a Spirit-filled believer is to be bound to other believers by peace, and to get firmer and stronger together, so that we all stand on our own two feet (Ephesians 4:2, 11–16). We're not looking to act more independently; instead, we're aiming to rest in dependence on God and interdependence with others, and from that deep sense of security, we are empowered to confidently take action. Far from being an unspiritual pursuit, looking for peace in our decisions requires us to walk with Jesus, the Prince of Peace. What deeper peace could we access than the peace he made by his sacrificial, reconciling love? He makes peace between God and people, and between people, and inside people. He quiets the war and hostility outside us and inside us.

Peace is an emotion, and it's a wonderful thing to feel. But it is also so much more. *Shalom* in the Bible is a term used to describe a reconciling peace for the person and for the whole community, a shared well-being and goodness and wholeness, a sense that things are working the way they should.

With this kind of peace inside of us because we have been reconciled with God, we're moved to make peace outside of us with others, to love our neighbor and our enemy. With this peace within us, we also worry less about what decisions are best for us, and we start being more concerned with making the kind of decisions that bring about God's peace in the world, especially in our small corner of the world. We keep looking and praying for God's kingdom of peace to come, on earth as it is in heaven, and this orientation transforms our quiet peace inside into an active peace outside. It moves our Sabbath into a week of new creation work. Instead of being immobilized with decision anxiety, we're mobilized toward God's work in the world. To be in this mindset is to be truly alive, as we were created to be.

STEWARDSHIP

We bring the peace of God into our role as managers, or "stewards," of our lives. In the Bible, a steward is someone who manages what belongs to someone else. This means that all we have is from God, and he has given us the calling and task of managing or governing what he has entrusted to us. Most of the time we probably don't feel like little kings and queens, ruling our worlds. We have overseers at work, at church, and in society. We often feel we don't have much power in our world. And it's true, we aren't equally responsible for everything in the same way, and not everything is ours only. It's a gift that we all aren't called to be in charge in every way.

But from another point of view, little kings and queens are exactly what we are. The picture that the book of Genesis paints of humanity includes images such as vice regents, royal gardeners, organizers, sorters, namers, and rulers. Humanity, at its ideal in Psalm 8, is a little lower than the angels, small in view of God but big in his world. People have all kinds of authority, managing and arranging every kind of animal in land and sky and sea. Of course, with evil in the picture, humanity is only a shell of its former self—sometimes more like the beasts than the angels.[2] Every day humans manage this world imperfectly, with staggeringly mixed results, curing diseases with one hand and turning away refugee children with the other. Stewardship matters; big decisions matter.

Every day humans manage their own little world with striking imperfection too. People take jobs they come to regret, date and marry against better judgment, and sometimes drive drunk. At the same time, as I write, some people are doing heroic and sacrificial work to provide health care in a global pandemic, some are dating and marrying with wisdom and kindness, and some are back to gathering in groups in church basements to help each other try to live sober. We are imperfect managers of a good but broken world. We are imperfect managers of good but broken lives. We do not have the option of perfect lives and perfect decisions. We often do not even have the full confidence that we've made the best decision out of the options available. We certainly do not know what the future holds. So what does God ask of his stewards, his managers of imperfect lives?

The apostle Paul gives us an idea. "This, then, is how you ought to regard us: as servants of Christ and as those entrusted with the mysteries God has revealed. Now it is required that those who have been given a trust must prove faithful" (1 Corinthians 4:1–2). God gives to his people a trust, a managerial oversight, and in this passage, the early leaders of the Christian faith wanted to faithfully manage their charge of teaching about the love of Jesus. By extension God also gives us a management of our own lives and areas of service. We don't outgrow the original calling of humanity in Genesis, to govern our little corner of the world, to order and arrange it so that it is fruitful (Genesis 1:28; Matthew 25:14–30).

Sometimes this feels like a lot to manage, and sometimes it feels like only a little. But no one else is ultimately responsible for my life in the way that I am—it's a special charge that we will give an account for (Romans 14:4, 12; 2 Corinthians 5:10). What is required of stewards is not to be perfect, to know the future, or to play the odds. We're called to be faithful. We will not always get it right, and not all situations even have a good solution. But every day we want to walk outside to the little plot of land that God has given us to garden. We water and fertilize, we tend and trim, and we trust God for fruit to come from our labors (1 Corinthians 3:6–8).

HOW THIS BOOK WILL HELP

This book won't provide you with a thorough protocol for making good decisions. I can't assure you of a great outcome for each of your decisions. I want to help you become freer from decision anxiety, and part of this freedom involves coming to terms with a difficult reality: for most of our nonmoral decisions, we don't have ultimate assurance that our decisions are good. Sometimes we don't even get reliable assurance that our decisions aren't bad. My goal is to help you live faithfully with these uncertainties.

Additional help is available in clear and accessible resources like Steven Johnson's *Farsighted*, which distills practical principles from a broader study of decision-making, whether for urban planning and corporate strategy or for personal decisions about career and romance.[3] Resources like this will help you make a better list of pros and cons prior to a significant decision, to add a numeric value to items on your list, to recognize knowns and unknowns, to think of the bigger picture and potential long-term consequences, to tolerate ambiguities and uncertainties, and to take constructive action. Many Christian resources draw from these kinds of practical strategies but also seek to add a fuller picture of the goals of a Christian's decision-making and help you toward a better understanding God's will. I'll highlight only one.

Much of the basic message for Christians about decision-making and God's will is captured in J. I. Packer's pamphlet, *Finding God's Will*.[4] He points out that we often encounter six key problems in times of decision-making. To work against each of these is to be freer to make good decisions:

1. unwillingness to *think*
2. unwillingness to *think ahead*
3. unwillingness to *take advice*
4. unwillingness to *suspect oneself*
5. unwillingness to *discount personal magnetism*
6. unwillingness to *wait*.[5]

By highlighting the value of thinking, Packer is pushing back against pietistic tendencies and toward reasoning with a conscience shaped by God's Word and values shaped by God's heart. By "unwillingness to discount personal magnetism," he identifies the problem of people coming under the sway of a compelling and domineering leader, and thus having their decision-making compromised and their decisions corrupted.

Most people will need messages like Packer's to grow in their discipleship as Christians. People who struggle with decision anxiety will also benefit from these broad resources but not yet. The reason is that those who struggle with decision anxiety are typically marked by a list of struggles that are the opposite of the six problems in Packer's list:

- overthinking
- thinking ahead so much that one isn't in the present
- gathering advice from as many people as possible
- feeling constant self-doubt and suspicion of oneself
- being unable to trust others
- delaying decisions so long that one loses opportunities

These problems make decisions quite difficult, and the more severe they are, the more paralyzed strugglers become. If they first turn to otherwise excellent resources like Packer's, they will likely become even more mired in decision anxiety. These kinds of struggles warrant some focused help. So I'll limit my focus to helping people who struggle with decision anxiety, whereas many other good books can help shape us as faithful decision-makers. One limitation of this short book is that I won't offer a comprehensive approach to decision-making, but helpful frameworks and general teaching can be found in resources listed at the end of this book.

HOW TO READ IN YOUR CONTEXT

I want to recognize other limitations as well. Culture heavily shapes the pressures and default protocols of decision-making. Although I have tried to expand my work so it can be applied in a variety of ways, my perspective is generally limited to my majority culture American context, which also describes most of the people I've served as a counselor during the past ten years. And yet, I do see many ways that culture directly impacts decision anxiety, so what I share will need to be worked out and adapted in individual and local contexts. For example, I find communal life to be anemic for many of the majority culture people who struggle with decision anxiety to whom I have provided counseling. Feeling alone and feeling great pressure to act, to self-create, to self-optimize, and to succeed in exceptional ways are significant contributing factors to anxiety.[6] Much of my guidance is shaped by providing care against this cultural backdrop. Those in other cultures may notice somewhat different challenges to their sense of peace and stewardship, and thus other contributing factors to their decision anxiety.

In some more collectivist cultures, the pressure to succeed may be expressed differently, but anxiety invades there too. Greg Jao highlights the difference between the US Army's tagline, "Be all that you can be," and the traditional Asian values that say, "Be all that your family has sacrificed for you to be."[7] In either case, the pressure to succeed, whether it's for self or for family, can be a significant contributor to decision anxiety. Our communities and cultures shape the contours of our pressures and anxieties. Other anxieties emerge in culture-specific ways as well, such as what Sheila Wise Rowe calls "breakaway guilt." Some young African Americans experience distress and anxiety about how educational and career decisions will impact their participation in the communities and relationships they grew up in, creating unique pressures on the decision-making process.[8]

Further, as you'll see especially in the chapters on marriage and vocation, our decisions largely flow from our sense of who we are and who we're called to be. Anxiety surrounding identity necessarily complicates decisions. In *Being Latino in Christ*, Orlando Crespo gives a window into identity confusion and formation,[9] and more recently, Robert Chao Romero captures the experience of liminality or in-betweenness in the American context, which fosters identity confusion and therefore makes many decisions more complex.[10]

Our sense of connection or disconnection from our communities, our sense of how we fit in and which culture we belong to, directly affects our ability to make big decisions—marriage, vocation, and location—but also smaller lifestyle choices. How we live is connected to who we are and who we want to be connected to. As Christians, we want our decisions to flow from who God has called us to be, and, ideally, we make these decisions within the church community as our most profound family. This can be a comforting message spiritually, but it can be a complicated message relationally. How can I make decisions when I face complications in asking who I am, who God has made me to be, and who he is calling me to be? How do I do this in the communities I live in, both family and church?

This leads us to the key messages in chapters 1 and 2 because these questions reveal, in part, how anxiety works: we become aware of ambiguity and uncertainty, we notice and react to the risk, and then our efforts to find certainty actually compound the problem. For believers, confusion about God's will further amplifies anxiety, so chapter 3 will complete part 1 on how anxiety works. We'll then consider where anxiety comes from—and how we come by it honestly. In chapters 4 and 5, we'll look at the kinds of pressures and messages from society and family that help us understand how easily decision anxiety can take hold, and why we get stuck while trying to make life decisions in young adulthood and beyond. Finally, we'll look at solutions through three examples: seeking prayerful knowledge of God and ourselves in anxiety about marriage (chapter 6), cultivating a mindset of stewardship in anxiety about career (chapter 7), and growing in the skill of Christian living by facing our fears in small decisions (chapter 8). This final chapter will engage more directly the kind of anxiety that can be described as OCD or scrupulosity, though this experience will also be touched on at various points throughout the book. Decision anxiety is not a technical term but an informal way to talk about anxiety that interferes with our decisions. Throughout the book, I will mostly use the language of the larger category of anxiety because most anxieties follow the same basic pattern.

Even so, there are no easy answers. I do believe, however, that the core messages of this book, at least to the extent that they reflect Christian concerns and hopes, will nudge us toward remembering a foundational biblical teaching that can bring us peace in a world of dangers: "God is our refuge and strength, an ever-present help in trouble" (Psalm 46:1).

QUESTIONS FOR REFLECTION

1. On a scale of 1 to 10 (1 being minimal, 10 being debilitating), how severe is your anxiety about decisions on most days?

2. What kinds of decisions often leave you feeling stuck?

3. This chapter contrasts two lists of problems with decisions. Which items on these lists most apply to you?

PART 1:
UNDERSTANDING
DECISION ANXIETY

Chapter 1

HOW DECISION ANXIETY WORKS

"A prudent person foresees danger and takes precautions." — Proverbs 27:12a (NLT)

Many times I've sat with people who broke down into tears over decisions. For some it was over things that others would see as the small stuff, like taking on a new regular volunteer opportunity or deciding how to spend a summer. It didn't feel small to them. They grieved because they saw the constant ruminating before and checking or regretting their decisions after were burdening or hurting people around them and complicating and stifling their own lives. They struggled to reach the assurance that it was okay to focus on one choice over another, one task over another, one project and not another, one career trajectory or another. *How could I ever know for sure what was best? Is anything less than that irresponsibility? How can I be sure?*

For others, it was late into the decision to get married, even after engagement. The anxiety remained intense, and the guilt and shame were overwhelming. Their minds raced with thoughts of embarrassment at explaining a potentially canceled wedding to extended relatives and lost deposits on venue and photographer. And then there are the thoughts and feelings for the other person that decision most affects. *How can I put my fiancé through this? How did I get here? What if I make a mistake on something this big?*

Maybe you get bogged down like this, too, in decisions that range from small and low-impact decisions to ones that alter the course of your whole life. Chances are, your decision anxiety follows the same basic contours: a feeling of being stuck, considering and reconsidering options, ruminating, getting advice, making a tentative decision, going back to a previously marked-off option, somehow stumbling through with a decision but then feeling regrets and lingering questions—all the while losing disproportionate time and feeling loads of distress.

In this chapter, we'll look at some of the basic patterns of anxiety. We'll look at how anxiety can become distorted into a larger way of navigating life that gets us stuck constantly seeking to eliminate risk and gets us locked down in a mode of ruminating. But first, let's start with how anxiety works when it is doing what it should—accurately signaling danger to us so that we can get to safety.

IT'S GOOD TO RECOGNIZE DANGER

Not all anxiety is a problem. If you are in a burning building, a spark of panic or fear motivates you to get out, and that's a good thing. When your brain doesn't register any fear, that's a bad thing. When it works the right way, anxiety—sensing danger—is God's gift to activate our bodies to move us to safety. Doing yard work, I have more than once come close to wasps' nests or snakes. My body generally does what it is supposed to do when that happens. It either freezes to stop and figure out a safe way forward, or it ramps itself up to fight off the danger or run away. That anxiety is pretty helpful. The alarm bells go off fast and loud, and that's what I need from my body. Our bodies activate when we sense danger of any kind. And that's a kindness from God in a fallen world.

Anxiety, however, doesn't usually feel like a gift. We read books like this because at least at some points in our lives, anxiety is a curse. Anxiety afflicts us, and it doesn't always reliably guide us away from danger. We need the capacity for anxiety as a built-in safety feature, but our bodies don't always work the way they should. We're kind of like houses with fire alarms. Most of us, mercifully, are only aware of our fire alarms when they are malfunctioning—whether it's chirping for new batteries or because they're too sensitive when you use the oven. Whatever the reason, when a fire alarm goes off, you can barely even hear yourself think. It is so loud that it dominates everything.

If you're just cooking, it's easy enough to find out whether or not there's a real, immediate danger. Other times it's less clear. If you're in a public building and you hear the alarm go off, you can't convince yourself that there's no fire, and really, you shouldn't. You know it's possible for a fire to really happen. You have to live with the possibility that the fire alarm really is picking up on a fire, and that it's not just a false alarm. The same is true for decision anxiety. We can't escape the fact that every time we make a decision, we face a real risk that we will make a bad choice or a decision that will result in negative consequences.

Because decisions always carry some risk, they should always carry a little anxiety, or at least a touch of caution. That's only wise because most decisions *could* end badly. Maybe there should be less anxiety for the less consequential decisions, but even those carry some risk.

Some people seem to not be terribly worried about big things going wrong because something deep inside them knows there are elements involved that can't be controlled, but then for little decisions, they give themselves no rest because those decisions, by contrast, feel all up to them. For example, I have to choose which route to drive home from one of our organization's counseling offices. Around rush hour, both routes have a similar ETA, but the highway is normally faster. So I ask, is the highway traffic going to clear, or will I be stuck for an hour if a truck has wrecked and blocked a section of road in the mountains? There's no guarantee which route is the best choice—I have only imperfect probabilities. There's always some uncertainty, risk, and the possibility that I'll regret my choice.

That is especially the case with the big fork-in-the-road decisions like career and marriage. Education can incur major debts, career direction can be hard to change, and marriage is for the long haul. These decisions continue throughout life: other large purchases can still incur debt, career moves can become only more complicated once the family is rooted somewhere, and deciding whether to remarry after loss is a massively complex decision. All these decisions require us to face risk.

ANXIETY'S GOAL: ELIMINATING RISK

Anxiety doesn't tolerate uncertainty and risk. Anxiety demands that you *know* you're safe. Anxiety is a mode of searching out uncertainties and gray areas and forcing those gray areas into black or white. *Is it safe or not? Do what you have to do to make it clearly safe.* When anxiety takes control, it becomes a mission to eradicate risk. That's especially true of the stereotypical obsessive-compulsive disorder (OCD) experience—washing hands, checking and rechecking locks, and much more. From an outside perspective, it's not hard to see that the guy who checks the lock on his front door multiple times each night isn't appreciably safer. But from the perspective of the guy overrun with this anxiety, you just need to know *for sure*. And you know memory isn't perfect. *What could ever be worth sacrificing the safety of your little children? Could you ever forgive yourself if a home invasion happened, and you just left the door wide open?* You see how this works. Once the doubt has even the smallest foothold, anxiety takes over. So you have to get rid of the risk.

When you begin to live dominated by the need to get rid of uncertainty and only make choices that don't involve risk, you gradually lose the ability to function in life. With severe decision anxiety, people typically don't seek help until the anxiety-relief strategies they engage in start to interfere with daily life:

- You lose hours at work because you're not sure you're focusing on the right task.
- You miss deadlines for selecting classes at college.
- You are late to your appointment because you got stuck trying to decide what to wear.
- You keep dating someone for years without being able to commit more seriously.

We usually can tolerate the small ways that anxiety inhibits us, but it can get to the point of exasperating ourselves and the people around us. Maybe you are the person who just can't pick something off the menu even after everyone else has ordered. Or you lose thirty minutes deciding which of the seven toilet flusher handles to buy at the hardware store. Some of us struggle to dismiss this kind of anxiety, even though we are aware *the whole time* that this small decision is not worth spending that much time on. This is what I call the one-two punch: anxiety and then self-loathing. "Oh no what should I do?" becomes "What's wrong with me?"

ANXIETY'S METHOD: RUMINATING

Sadly, the many things we do to reduce anxiety only make it worse. Decision anxiety keeps itself going by ruminating. Most anxious thoughts start with identifiable phrases like "What if" or "Should I" or "Maybe I":

- What if I get into this job and hate it?
- Should I really be spending my time on this rather than that?
- Maybe I'm just in this relationship because I'm afraid of being alone.

"What if" is probably the dominant look and feel. *What if I've missed something? I'm an imperfect decider. What if I'm being selfish? What if God is moving me in one of these directions and I'm not listening?* All fair questions, in theory, but they can paralyze people with a scrupulous conscience and become part of the never-ending obsessiveness and fearful rumination of decision anxiety. This kind of questioning is different from open-handed spiritual reflection. It is different from the trusting posture, or a time-limited season of prayerful self-examination, of considering where we might be wrong or shortsighted or overly self-oriented. People who haven't experienced more severe decision anxiety will sometimes struggle to understand how this works.

The reason people race through these thoughts is actually *to get rid of* anxiety. The reason to mentally race back through the decision-making process—to re-ask the same questions or reexamine the alternatives or relist the pros and cons or ask yet another friend for an opinion—is to try to eliminate the danger. Anxious thoughts are excellent at locating potential dangers. The problem is that ruminating can't fix the dangers it finds. It finds risk or uncertainty and tries everything possible to reduce or eliminate it. But it's like rubbing your eye when it is irritated. You feel like something is in your eye, so you instinctively put your hand there. But of course, it only introduces more irritants or moves around what was already in there, bothering your eye even more. Tragically, assurance-seeking strategies for dealing with decision anxiety leave us with even more anxiety. That's the experience of nervously trying to manage life with severe decision anxiety. It just keeps getting worse.

QUESTIONS FOR REFLECTION

1. What risks seem to be the most difficult for you to accept or live with?

2. Anxiety often leads to self-criticism or self-loathing. Are you regularly berating yourself, leaving out grace in your inner monologue in a way that you don't when you speak words aloud to others?

Chapter 2

WHY TRYING TO FIX ANXIETY DOESN'T WORK: FOUR WAYS WE MAKE IT WORSE

"Something must die in order for the new self to be born, and it might be an old self to which we are very attached." - Rebecca Konyndyk DeYoung[1]

The first step in getting past decision anxiety is to stop using the old ways we've tried to find rest. Sometimes the things we lean on cannot hold us. In 2 Kings 18:21 we read these surprisingly wise words spoken by an enemy of God's people: "Look, I know you are depending on Egypt, that splintered reed of a staff, which pierces the hand of anyone who leans on it! Such is Pharaoh king of Egypt to all who depend on him." We can likewise seek the wrong kind of assurance, safety, and support by leaning on a walking stick that can't hold us up, one that pierces our hand. Strategies for reducing anxiety don't help in the way we hope they would and, in the end, actually accelerate anxiety.

It's here that decision anxiety can fit several of the criteria of OCD. The OCD response to anxiety works like this: people with an extreme fear of germs can wash their hands over and over and construct increasingly elaborate showering or vacuuming and disinfecting rituals.

Similarly, people who struggle with decision anxiety can have a whole set of counterproductive practices they use to seek assurance.

OVERTHINKING

Decision anxiety and ruminating are almost synonymous. One of the most common problems in decision-making is the inability to narrow down options. Or some of us narrow our options, but then we find that we keep adding them back to the list. The etymology of the word *decision* is to "cut off," and how fitting the word's history is—when making a decision, it is both necessary and painful to cut off options. Decision anxiety locks in on the risk of letting go of a good option, insisting that we revisit options that we had previously removed from the list. Or if we do make a decision, we struggle to stick with it. Our decisions live under perpetual review. As one researcher says, "overthinking is often the enemy of a satisfactory conclusion."[2]

OVERCONSULTING

Decision anxiety leads us toward leaning too heavily on the opinions of others. Of course, sometimes you do get advice that is just pure gold. You hit on something extremely valuable in a friend's knowing, insightful comment. But usually, our wise friends function more like road signs, lines, and guardrails: useful, vital, and protective, but they can't ultimately tell you which direction you need to go.

The reason we can become overreliant on others is because we don't trust ourselves to make a good decision. We feel the weight of having the role of decision-maker, and something deep inside wishes that just maybe someone else might be willing to step in and make the call. On the one hand, it sounds really spiritual *not* to trust our-selves. On the other hand, many of our decisions are truly ours and not someone else's. And if God alone deserves our ultimate trust, then we can't rest fully either on our-selves or on other people. We're left with the responsibil-ity of prayerful discernment, with God and others, and then the obligation to make our decisions.

The scary, practical reality is that it feels like God puts enormous decisions into our hands. And that can be heavy to bear. So we absolutely want to bear this burden with others and turn away from overdependence without overcorrecting to extreme independence and individual-istic living. We want to break the cycle of obsessive con-sulting, which looks like this: you reach out to others, and then when the sense of risk doesn't go away, you keep on reaching out, too many times to too many people. I have known people paralyzed because their advisers have dif-ferent opinions, and the person feels stuck in the middle. The tragedy here is that we can exhaust all of our friends, family, and mentors and still in the end feel more alone and confused than ever.

OVERCHECKING

Related to overthinking, one mark of decision anxiety is to overcheck or overmonitor whatever risk indicators we have. Usually this includes the wrong kind of interest in emotion. On the one hand, many Christians need to pay better attention to emotions. Lots of things go wrong when we never stop to think about how we feel. We're not, as James K. A. Smith likes to say, "brains on a stick."[3] But on the other hand, when we have decision anxiety, monitoring our emotions too closely can create more prob-lems. This gets even more complicated by the belief that

God primarily leads us to wise decisions through impressions and felt assurances, which we will explore further in chapter 3. Emotions are often helpful indicators, but they are our reaction to the world, guided by how we interpret our world and what we value.[4] So emotions can tell us something but not everything, and often not enough in themselves to be a clear or decisive guide.

The key problem with overchecking is that it takes us away from life in the here and now, and we get lost in our heads. This can look like constantly monitoring how you feel about your internship or college major or thinking too much in real-time about whether you're really enjoying the date that you're on. It's possible to so frequently check for assurance that we aren't able to engage what's right in front of us.

Anxiety makes it hard to focus on the here and now, leading us away from where God has called us today. These fears can also drive the desire to escape the hard work of making decisions.

OVERESCAPING

Decision anxiety is essentially an effort at avoiding risks that can't be totally avoided. Sometimes that avoidance looks like a football player running at full speed, spinning, stiff-arming, and evading tackles. Sometimes that avoidance looks like not stepping onto the field at all. Of course, the stereotypical avoidance strategies include phone-scrolling, shopping, and video games. But really it can involve anything other than the work of the hard decision. It's similar to what the medieval Christians called *acedia*. It's usually translated sloth, but it doesn't necessarily mean laziness. Usually it involves doing something, just not the spiritual task at hand. This is why, as many have pointed out, being a workaholic or couch potato can both stem from the same issue—avoidance.[5] The best description I've heard is that *acedia* is "resistance to the demands of love."[6] A key move away from anxiety is to pursue the opposite: Who is God calling me to love? What does this call require of me today?

Decision anxiety usually feels like an experience of suffering, but to bring in the language of love may make it sound moral. Is decision anxiety a sin, too, if it resists the demands of love of God and our neighbor? If your friend at dinner is stuck between menu choices and holding up the order, you're probably not feeling wronged in any meaningful sense. Irritated, maybe, though in view of what you've read so far in this book, you might feel compassion. But that compassion for the anxious usually runs out when you see a friend dating someone who avoids a decision on commitment. The person they're dating is nice enough, but weeks turn into months and years of a relationship that never reaches a conclusion. It's much harder to be compassionate toward a person's decision anxiety when it's so deeply hurting one of your dear friends. Or perhaps you're the person who maintains multiple options for too long. What tends to drive this? I know one pastor who calls it "the idolatry of options." And he probably has a point. Ancient cultures built idols and maintained practices to appease the gods and keep them safe from wars or crop failures. We're not ultimately all that different. A biblical understanding of sin is not just willful pleasure-seeking at the expense of others. Often we do damage by turning to the wrong things when we are afraid. We hold onto unloving practices that help us feel safe. But any false refuge ultimately doesn't keep ourselves or other people safe.

Maintaining options and delaying decisions gives a false sense of safety. In contrast, good decision-makers seem to set time limits for themselves, or at least they don't let the decision-making process go on indefinitely. If you wait long enough, options will start dropping off, and that can make the decision easier. But really this is a form of self-sabotage. The clock won't necessarily make better decisions than we will, and we don't escape the possibility that we'll still have lots of regrets and what ifs to look back on because of the lost options.

You may have experienced other marks of decision anxiety. Most are forms of avoidance or escape. I know of some people who always try to choose the safest option because it feels wise. But the downside of this default process is that it makes life quite small—and it requires no faith. I know of others who feel like they should choose the least pleasant option because it seems like it might be the godliest option. At least then they would know they weren't being selfish and just trying to avoid suffering. All these methods or formulas create the illusion of escaping the act of making a decision. But all of these efforts to avoid risk ultimately fail. And they don't necessarily lead to better decisions. So how will God meet us in this?

Pray with me that God will unravel what keeps us tied down and anxious and interrupt the practices that maintain our intolerance of uncertainty. Pray he will guide us toward places of rest and refuge in the presence of risk. In the next section, we'll look at several of the common arenas for decision anxiety and how to not only avoid making it worse but how to make concrete changes for the better.

QUESTIONS FOR REFLECTION

1. Which of the four strategies listed do you find your-self gravitating toward?

2. Anxiety makes our world small and inward-focused. Who has God placed in your life that you feel bur-dened to care for in this season? What good things might you have desire or ambition to do if you were freer from anxiety?

3. This chapter framed risk-avoiding strategies as a form of seeking safety or refuge. Take a moment to talk to God, asking him to draw near and be a comfort through the moments of anxiety and struggle.

Chapter 3

FEELING MIXED UP ABOUT GOD'S WILL

"God in his providence doesn't reveal the fullness of our lives. Instead, he gives it to us moment by moment, in small doses that we can metabolize and handle." — D. Michael Lindsay[1]

Anxiety about decisions is hard on its own, but sometimes confusion about God's will makes the experience even worse. This spiritualized amplification of anxiety is particularly tragic because the people who struggle in this way are typically sensitive, soft-hearted believers. It occurs only when a person is concerned about God's desires and plans. But the distress increases when they don't see a clear answer about what it is God wants them to do, whether in big or small decisions. The heart in this distress is, "Lord, I'll do whatever it is you call me to do, but please show me what that is!" So what does God want us to know, and how do we navigate our decisions in light of it?

From one theological perspective, Christians believe that God tells us his *moral will*. That means that he tells us in the Bible how to worship him, love our neighbor, do good, and avoid sin. But God does not tell us other aspects of his will that some call his *secret will*. This means we do not know (at least not usually) what God wants us to do with nonmoral decisions—decisions where the available options are not in themselves right or wrong, such as which specific college we should attend or whether we should buy the T-shirt on sale. Those decisions can involve gradations of more or less wisdom or purity of motivation, but we don't know which decision is the one we should make by the available alternatives alone. Or, to say it another way, we know the moral principle not to steal, so when presented with the opportunity to commit theft, we know which decision is the right one to make. In contrast, with nonmoral decisions, we won't know only by looking at the options which is right and which is wrong—we don't know for certain whether we should buy a house or rent because neither choice is morally wrong in itself.

I think this perspective on God's will is basically the right approach to take, while also leaving some room for what my denomination's statement of faith says about how God works: "God, in His ordinary providence, maketh use of means, yet is free to work without, above, and against them, at His pleasure."[2] God sometimes works in unexpected ways to accomplish his will. Leaving room for this reminds us that we don't have everything about God buttoned up, pinned down, or in a box.[3] He surprises us, and we all know this. Even the most anticharismatic Christian takes note and prays for wisdom when a decision doesn't feel right and still prays for healing when a loved one is sick (James 1:5; 5:14–16). We know how things ordinarily work, but we still pray for God to do special things. Sometimes he does. With health and with our decisions, we don't always see God working a miracle or suspending the normal course of events in response to what we might ask and long for. But we still ask because we care and we know that God cares too.

I want to be clear that sincere believers differ on some of these things. Many Christian writers from a more mystical tradition have left much to us that is valuable. And today, fellow believers have much to offer us, and we should expect to challenge and refine one another. Some have more confidence about knowing God's specific desires for their lives, and some have less confidence that this is how God typically works. Many believers are confident they have discerned God's will for some of their decisions and less so for some of their other decisions—when they are confident, they see God as the ultimate source of their clarity. Regardless of where you fall in this continuum, Christians do believe that God is, in a mysterious way, involved in the details of their lives. Although I believe God leads us and gives us clarity in the Bible on how to live, our felt impressions are not a reliable way to discern the right course of specific, nonmoral actions.[4] That also doesn't mean feelings are in some special way deceptive or unreliable or that being more ostensibly rational or logical is a more certain guide to wisdom. Feelings like confidence, conviction, concern, and compassion are all emotions that, rightly ordered, play an important role in our decisions. Often, however, we have to act without feelings of full confidence or feelings of certainty. Often we have to take a step of faith and entrust the results to God.

Another way to describe this trust is *risk*. I will probably not think to pray, "O Lord, help me trust you in this," if I have not first experienced the feeling of risk or danger. And for people who struggle with anxiety, risk feels like the great enemy to be avoided at all costs. Trust is essential to the Christian life, but it can be really uncomfortable. The problem is that anxiety naturally nudges us *away* from trust because it feels like risk. And we tell ourselves lots of messages about God and his will that help us avoid risk.

The theologian Herman Bavinck points out two extremes to avoid when you try to understand how God gives grace to us: the "mystical" and the "magical" views.[5] Although Bavinck doesn't have decisions primarily in mind, I believe he gives us a helpful analogy for God's guidance. In the mystical view, we undervalue the ordinary ways God gives us wisdom or guidance. We prefer the idea that he might give it to us directly. In the magical view, we overvalue the avenues of wisdom and guidance, often privileging one above the other, and treating them as though they work like an incantation, a spell, or a vending machine.

MYSTICAL

In the mystical view, the idea is that God has not already provided us with all the resources we need to make wise and faithful nonmoral decisions, but he may tell us more directly which decision to make if we open ourselves up to him, fully surrender, and wait on him. A common practice within the mystical view is to create tests or circumstances, based on the biblical example of Gideon's fleece (see Judges 6:36–40), to receive direct guidance from God. This approach carries the danger of devaluing the ways God already helps us make decisions—discernment, advice from other wise believers, and biblical principles—because we want him to directly give us an answer, without mediation or the ordinary ways we gain wisdom. The fact that God granted Gideon's request should be seen more as generous accommodation than affirmation of the method of putting out the fleece. This desire for direct guidance from God is a form of mysticism. Usually this means looking for a set of feelings or signs we think may be from God, so they help us make the right decision.

It's wise to be cautious about assuming our feelings are God's leading, but we also can't ignore or discount feelings entirely. Sometimes our feelings are saying something to us about ourselves that we aren't yet ready to accept. For example, a common phrase during a Christian breakup is that "I just didn't feel peace about moving forward with the relationship." That can be Christian-speak for "I don't want to date you, and I don't want to say why" or "I don't want to date you, and I haven't yet figured out why." Acting on those feelings is not necessarily a bad thing. Feeling out of sorts or not peaceful can be really important because sometimes it comes from a whole list of half-forgotten, unsettling things that have accumulated over time. For example, maybe it didn't sit right with you how your boyfriend talks to other women. Or it didn't sit right with you how your girlfriend reacted when she found out you were, at best, a B student. And then maybe fifty other really small things happened, and you haven't yet figured out the words to say why you're just not feeling at home or comfortable or connected.

Feelings don't outright tell you God's will, at least not in a way you can be certain about. However, it's ultimately loving to make the hard call and break up (politely but clearly) if you don't feel that it's a good fit. You may not have direct leading from God on whether to break up, but you *can* know it's God's will to do the loving thing. And if you really want to grow in the skill of decision-making, you must get used to experiencing some measure of discomfort during and after the decision-making process.

I've emphasized the basic helpfulness of feelings in decision-making. But the opposite can also be true—our feelings can profoundly mislead us. I've previously written and spoken on marital restoration after infidelity, and though there is more to it, it is also not an oversimplification to say that affairs typically come from following or avoid-ing certain feelings.[6] Esther Perel captures the experience powerfully in "Why Happy People Cheat."[7] Sometimes God's guidance runs counter to our desires and feelings, and other times our emotions are more in tune with God's heart; in those cases, we find ourselves desiring what is good and hating what is bad. Our emotions, like every part of us, are in the process of spiritual formation. They are imperfect responses to our world. So in decision-making, engaging with our emotions requires discernment.

An alternative to the mystical view is to see God as only directly telling us what he most wants us to know in his Word, which the Holy Spirit illuminates and helps us understand, interpret, and apply in community with other believers. The Holy Spirit guides us toward mature stewardship of sometimes hard decisions. As we steward our choices, his Word and the godly counsel of other believers must be close at hand. We also consider our preferences and feelings, but we don't treat them as direct revelation from God. All these things are valuable sources of information and wisdom, and this is the help God ordinarily uses to help us make decisions. In the con-text of decision anxiety, we might say that God gives us grace through his Word, wise friends, prayer, reflection, and, yes, even feelings. We do not want to be mystical in undervaluing his kindnesses for us, his means of grace. At the same time, we also do not want to overvalue or isolate any one of these gifts as uniquely determinative for non-moral decisions, as we do when we hold the magical view.

MAGICAL

The magical view attaches clear divine authority to the kind gifts of wisdom and guidance from God, often focusing on one in particular. The magical view overvalues a good thing. It can look like a young man pointing back to a church service where he felt that God used a sermon to convincingly call him to be a missionary. Or a friend gave strong feedback, and it brought a definite sense of confidence that seemed to be from God. It is easy to cling to a sign or signal and overinflate it to be a primary source of confidence, so we don't have to live with the anxiety of having made a decision. Sometimes life can be so confusing that we long to have something steady to hang onto. This is an understandable desire, but we must make sure we're hanging onto the right things.

The biblical prophet Jeremiah preaches against finding a false sense of safety in a symbol of God's presence, which was, in this case, the Israelites' proximity to God's temple: "Do not trust in deceptive words and say, 'This is the temple of the LORD, the temple of the LORD, the temple of the LORD!'" (Jeremiah 7:4). It was not wrong to think of God's blessings in connection with the presence of the temple. But because they were tolerating all kinds of sin and injustice, their sense of safety was improperly founded. Similarly, we may not be wrong to think of God as in some sense guiding us through a particular sermon or a friend's affirmation or some other experience. But those cannot be, in themselves, a place of safety that protects us from risk or trust.

What the Lord wants is holy living before him and fellowship with him. He wants us not to cling to any refuge outside of himself. With nonmoral decisions, no single verse, no internal experience, no affirmation from others or confluence of events could be enough so that we can point to it and say, "This is no longer my decision. Take it up with God, he did this." This level of responsibility is sobering to consider. God is leading us toward stewardship. It can be uncomfortable to find ourselves entrusted with these things, and yet this is not a mistake. Even in a broken world, this is what we were made for, and as believers, God provides for us what we need to do it faithfully: "His divine power has given us everything we need for a godly life through our knowledge of him who called us by his own glory and goodness" (2 Peter 1:3).

When decisions are difficult and consequential, it's understandable to anxiously search for God's guidance, to want a reliable path or protocol that will give us a sense of peace. To have God's secret, specific will or instructions revealed in this way feels secure; it feels like a guaranteed way to avoid the risk of a bad decision. It's hard to live with the reality that we don't know all we'd like to know before we make decisions, and that in most nonmoral decisions, we won't ultimately know with perfect assurance we're making the right decision, or the decision that will lead to the outcomes we desire.

The value in reflecting on ways we misunderstand God's will and guidance is that it brings us more quickly to a place of desperation, dependence, and rest. When we still believe there's a way to avoid risk in decision-making, our anxieties will be quite active. But to let go of our desire to avoid all risks is to take a good step toward a walk of faith.

We've now finished considering how decision anxiety works for many believers. We experience risk, danger, and uncertainty, and we try to eliminate them. But because that's not possible, we find ourselves stuck in anxiety that compounds the harder we try to get rid of it. And for some believers, this anxiety compounds even further because we are confused about God's will and we fear missing his direction. The alternative—childlike trust—feels risky, but it is ultimately safest to be leaning only on the Father in heaven. In part 2, we'll look at two places where we learn to be anxious. Just as unlearning the risk-avoidant strategies we looked at in part 1 will help us start to defeat decision anxiety, unlearning the messages we've picked up from society and family will take us to the next step in moving toward hearing God's truth, and trusting his words over the messages that stoke anxiety.

QUESTIONS FOR REFLECTION

1. Which of the perspectives that this chapter examined has influenced your understanding of God's will? Do you have concerns about the will of God that affect your ability to make decisions?

2. If you find this chapter persuasive, how might your view of God's will change? How might this change your experience of decision-making?

PART 2:
WHERE DECISION
ANXIETY COMES FROM

Chapter 4

NAVIGATING A CULTURE OF FEAR IN YOUNG ADULTHOOD AND BEYOND

"I just assumed you'd get to a certain age and everything would make sense. Bless my young little heart. . . . My ducks are not in a row, they are wandering." — Maria Eleusiniotis[1]

In part 1 we looked at how anxiety can plague our hearts and minds, generally focusing on what was happening within us. In part 2 we look now to the ways that anxiety is learned, or strengthened, by messages coming from outside of us, specifically from culture and family. There's no one script for decision anxiety, or one set of messages or experiences that guarantees a person to struggle in this specific way, but there do seem to be trends. And although we are always interpreting and responding to the messages we receive, there's value in considering how we learned where to direct our worries. Sometimes we aren't as effective in holding on to the truth until we see the ways we've been lied to. Or, at least, we find ourselves always having perspectives, values, or scripts that have biases and imbalances we learned in family life and in our broader culture.

One such script is the coming-of-age process. A society's general rules for growing up and gaining independence are a significant arena for decision anxiety. Every society has coming-of-age rituals. By participating in them, we learn what it means to be a grown-up, and we mutually reinforce the various benchmarks. Most of these benchmarks of adulthood, at least in the United States, are steps of independence. You get a learner's permit then a license. You go on a first date. You go to college. You live on your own. You get a job. Some even feel like they won't be treated as adults until they get married or have children. That feeling of uneasiness or insecurity about whether you've finally made it to adulthood doesn't necessarily go away on its own. Some joke about being in their fifties and wondering what they'd like to do when they grow up. What it means to become an adult can be a bit fuzzy. Beyond this, it can be a challenge at any age to know how to carry responsibility and make wise decisions. But the pressure is especially heavy on young adults. Cultural dynamics exist that intensify anxiety for many.

ANXIETY AND EMERGING ADULTHOOD

In the year 2000, two major studies were released that indicated children in the 1950s reported significantly less anxiety than children in the 1980s.[2] And in the years since then, available metrics suggest a continued and significant rise in anxiety of young people in particular, especially high school and college students.[3] The sociologist Anthony Giddens says that anxiety is rising in society because we've lost our traditional sources of identity—family, church, and community. For many of us, these traditional authorities don't tell us who we are or where our place is in the world, at least not in the way they once did. Your job isn't automatically decided by what your parents' jobs were. The community isn't really involved in helping you get married. You most likely feel like it is up to you to discover who you are and then figure out what kinds of decisions fit with the kind of person you've identified yourself as. And, especially in the majority culture in the United States, young adulthood is the time to explore these questions. It's normal to waffle a bit, to try several different jobs, relationships, or locations. This time of life is characterized by a lot of uncertainty, compounded by a sense that even the exploratory decisions matter, that they're consequential. This pressure makes landing in any one place difficult. Hesitation, concern, and some degree of instability are common.

This instability makes young adulthood an easy punching bag. It's not hard to shame the stereotypical young man living in his parents' basement, playing video games and putzing around in the general direction of a career. Perhaps you've heard popular pastors say that we need to get rid of "adultolescence" and make boys, in particular, grow up sooner. Thinly veiled exasperation is the undertone when some talk about "kids these days." From this vantage point, young adults are not growing up fast enough—they're struggling to hit cultural benchmarks of adulthood like marriage, career, or home ownership.

If you've heard and internalized shaming messages like these, I want to offer you another perspective. Cultural benchmarks are changing. People are getting married later. Most adults under thirty-five do not own their home. Career trajectories are changing. Work is just different now. Few employees or employers have the mutual expectation of developing careers over decades in the same company. Larger forces like recessions and college debt have also been in the picture. The old script of how to grow up and live the good life doesn't work the same way in a new context, and this increases uncertainties and creates new pressures.

There are also unhelpful cultural messages about growing up. Coming of age is almost exclusively understood in the majority culture as an individual, isolated, independent thing. You do it on your own, and your success or failure is your glory or shame. But it is up to you. As Christians, we're vulnerable to all these messages, but we're also vulnerable to the simplistic pushbacks and reactions against those messages, their mirror-image errors. I never found Christian messages against "prolonged adolescence" personally helpful. The messages are condescending, and even some of the names given to the life stage are pejorative.

But they're not wrong about adolescence being prolonged. There is something *like* adolescence going on in those years, roughly between eighteen and thirty. Some who study human development say that this stage, "emerging adulthood[,] is much like adolescence, only with less scaffolding."[4] Much of life can still feel unsettled and out of sorts, but there is less help and structure for getting settled and sorted. It's not clear to me that the existence of this stage in our current cultural moment is an entirely bad thing, and though not all agree that it can be well defined, it appears to be a thing. So whether a culture recognizes our full adulthood at eighteen, twenty-eight, or fifty-eight, it is important to reorient ourselves to a biblical picture of growing up spiritually and draw implications from it for growing up in other ways. Christian maturity is a strong antidote to decision anxiety.

GROWING UP SPIRITUALLY

The goal in Ephesians 4 is that all of us will achieve maturity in Christ so that we are no longer children. Although we never outgrow our need for God our Father, we don't stay infants or little children. We grow up spiritually, which means we're less tossed around by bad ideas (v. 14), we reach a spiritual stability, and we get stronger. And God, especially through the church, gives us just what we need to grow. In Ephesians 4:15–16, as we are "speaking the truth in love, we are to grow up in every way into him who is the head, into Christ, from whom the whole body, joined and held together by every joint with which it is equipped, when each part is working properly, makes the body grow so that it builds itself up in love" (ESV). This is described in verse 13 as mature adulthood (a form of *telos*), which is a good translation, but there may be a bit more to it. When God finishes growing us up, making us mature, he's bringing us to our goal and intended purpose. Maturity is not just hitting certain benchmarks or reaching certain stages of life; it is becoming who we are intended to be in Christ.

Christians believe that the redemptive love of God invites us to a glory and goodness we can only dream of, a day when the things that could rightly be called spiritual immaturity go away and a rich Christian maturity is fully here—a steadiness, a sense of clear direction, a deep knowledge that who we are is what we are created to be, a person fully alive to God. We get that only imperfectly here and now, but we do get it. You'll see it in moments when you decide to do the right thing, even if it might carry a consequence. You see it when you make a hard decision, and no one else will know that you denied yourself something you wanted but that was wrong, unloving, or selfish. You see it in moments when you don't desire glory for yourself, but when you make a decision out of your freedom to serve the Lord with gladness, to love your neighbor and even your enemy.

Reoriented in this way to a fuller vision of spiritual maturity, we see the anxieties about making grown-up decisions differently. We still struggle when we feel stuck in a career or stalled in a potential romantic relationship. We still feel the confusion and regret of having to switch college majors or making a car purchase that turns out poorly. We still feel frustrated when we don't know which next step to take, and when it's the kind of choice that no one else can make for us.

All that can still happen, and it is never pleasant. But what a beautiful thing it is to be deeply at peace, to be spiritually steady, to be loving and serving others even when you feel stuck, to be able to take small, constructive steps even when you feel confused or anxious. You don't necessarily access any hidden knowledge about what car is really best to buy or what college major is optimal. But you do find that the goal of maturing in Christ, of being more like him, makes the many decisions more manageable. Instead of trying to live up to cultural standards of maturity (many of which you may not be able to achieve because of factors outside your control), you can instead focus your sight on becoming mature according to spiritual goals. As a result, you're freer to faithfully endure what is not in your power and to engage well what is in your power. This kind of spiritual maturity steadies you through the inevitable gray areas, the uncertainties, the ambiguous options that happen throughout life. And it's a beautiful thing to see. It's a sweet testimony of what Jesus does in your life.

SPIRITUAL MATURITY AT ANY AGE

Emerging adulthood is a particularly challenging time for decision anxiety. Living in a culture where big life decisions and identity formation rest on the choices of the individual fosters these anxieties. But decisions don't necessarily get less complex when a spouse or children are in the picture or when singleness is our calling in middle age or our older years. For some, the sense of isolation, the feeling that everything is up to you, only intensifies after multiple relocations, after job or church changes, or after lost friendships. If anything, distance from friends and family can increase after young adulthood, and many anxieties intensify because we face them in greater isolation. Vivek Murthy, a former surgeon general, spoke of an epidemic of loneliness even prior to the global pandemic.[5] The pressure on the isolated individual to self-define and self-direct is significant in emerging adulthood, but these same pressures show up in other life stages. And so does anxiety.

So I want to give you a few simple ways to push back against the pressures toward individual achievement and success that so complicate our decisions and infuse us with insecurity. I hesitate to say these are especially important for young adults because each one is important across the life span.

- Avoid the comparison game. We're all falling behind someone. The goal is simply to walk faithfully with Jesus today.
- If you're on social media, take regular breaks for parts of every day, week, month, and year. There seems to be a connection between spending lots of time on social media and anxiety.[6]
- Spend time with people as a discipline, and find friends who help you stay focused on what really matters. Push back against conversations that tempt you toward misguided values, whether it's humble brags, vacations, or diet plans.

• Start practicing a real Sabbath of worship, rest, and only tasks that are acts of service or necessity.

I have given only a few to start with, but the principles underlying these small ways to start are simple: be connected to God and to others in edifying ways, practice rhythms of connection and quietness, and live humbly but generously within your God-given limits. Think of someone you consider a spiritually mature Christian whose decisions you admire. Almost certainly, you'll see these principles at work.

Spiritual maturity, a posture of resting with Jesus, can take us through seasons of "growing up" or difficult transitions at any age, holding us steady amid cultural messages that place tremendous pressure on the isolated individual to figure out life. We don't have to go it alone. Speaking the truth in love to each other, we hold each other together through the things that resist figuring out, and even through the things that we never quite figure out. The gifts of God sustain us even there. And he can redirect us amid other powerful and confusing influences, some of which we'll examine in the next chapter.

QUESTIONS FOR REFLECTION

1. In what ways are you finding "adulting," or making grown-up choices, to be wearisome or anxiety inducing?

2. What restorative practices of rest and connection to God and others can you begin making time for?[7]

3. How are you doing with your connection to others? Do your primary companions enhance or reduce your insecurities? What do they point you toward?

Chapter 5

HOW OUR FAMILIES TEACH US WHAT TO FEAR AND WHY IT'S SO PERSUASIVE

"If you hold to my teaching, you are really my disciples. Then you will know the truth, and the truth will set you free." — John 8:31b-32

Christians generally like the idea of the family being responsible for shaping most of how we view the world. Better that than cable news, we might say. But the messages we receive in family life can shape us in both helpful and unhelpful ways. Our families are our own little world when we are young, and we learn about what the big world is like through this little world we live in. Our family culture affects how we view ourselves in the world and how we engage with our world as decision-makers. This is not to say that all our bad ideas or fears are someone else's fault. It also doesn't mean that we aren't responsible for what we do with the messages we grow up hearing and believing. I only mean that fears develop in a context. Understanding the context that shaped some of the contours of your anxieties will help you find the way out and will shed new light on life-giving, biblical messages.

HOW FAMILY CAN COMPLICATE OUR DECISION-MAKING

There are two ways to talk about family life that aren't ultimately helpful. In the first way, it's said that because no one's family is perfect it's best to get on with life rather than blaming. The second is that your family's problems more or less explain everything important about you. Neither one quite captures reality. You can't brush off family influences, but there's also more to you than what's happened in your family life. What your parents did or failed to do isn't the only reason decision-making might be hard, but family influences probably play a big part.

In the previous chapter, I considered it a cultural loss that family and community play such a minimal role in helping young adults navigate life decisions. Pressure on the isolated individual fosters anxiety. But family life during one's childhood can also cultivate anxiety. It can influence or motivate us to be confident and to believe we have the ability to make a difference in our world. Or it can push us to avoid conflict, to avoid disappointing others, and to fear that we are not capable or trustworthy people.

I'll start with one example of how a family environment can significantly influence a person's ability to make decisions. Consider the example of a person who grew up in a home where several family members were a little too free with critical words and feelings of irritation. The small bumps in the road of daily life could unsettle those who were more reactive, and so if a person was not similarly reactive, it was not hard to develop a way of life oriented toward taking care of others' feelings. Concerns for maintaining a sense of calm and predictability came to drive more of the big and little decisions. Perhaps, if this is a story you resonate with, you lived with a heightened awareness of how irritable or reactive people in your household responded to your decisions, and you learned that looking at life from the perspective of others made aspects of life easier and smoother. You wanted to anticipate and avoid things that might unsettle. So, even though you grew up and left the house eventually, in the back of your head, you may still hear the kinds of critical words you grew up with when you order off a menu or pick out clothes. You don't expect people to be gracious and understanding, so it's natural to consistently live just a bit on guard.

When you filter your decisions through the potential reactions of others, and feel unsteady about making decisions, we can call this effect a loss of *agency*. And in more extreme situations, you don't feel like you can make your own choices, or at least not well, because you've come to believe that you regularly make bad decisions. That's likely especially true if you were told that explicitly. And so feelings of powerlessness set in, and you don't feel like you are someone who can accomplish things, big or small. When you do make a choice, especially if it is one that affects other people, you question it and you may look at others' reactions to define how you should feel about that decision.

Diane Langberg ties this idea of agency, or in her words, power, to the image of God in us. In the context of her focus area of service, she says that the ongoing mistreatment of children tears down our God-given agency. It takes away our power, along with the God-given sense of voice and the ability to relate to others in the ways we otherwise would.

If God created you to take the mindset of a steward or manager toward your life and decisions (and he did), then it has to get broken down or compromised in some way for it not to function.[1] It doesn't take outright violence or an abusive environment to accomplish this. There are other ways to lose the sense that you have meaningful dominion over your small corner of creation, or that God has truly given you the capacity to make sensible and trustworthy decisions.

A less extreme version of this loss of agency can occur with "helicopter parents" who hover close and oversee and assist with every detail of life for their kids, even during the teen and young adult years. More recently, parenting scholars have identified a trend they call "bulldozer" parenting, where parents get rid of obstacles, make big decisions for their older kids, and accomplish tasks for them, clearing the way for their success. You can imagine that this kind of attitude toward parenting doesn't foster in children a sense of agency and confidence that they can set good goals, make hard decisions, and accomplish things; rather, well-meaning parents may by their very efforts inhibit these important attributes from developing.

It does not require extreme problems in parenting for a person to develop decision anxiety. Imagine yourself as a person who has a sensitive temperament, and also has spent lots of time around a person with quite a dominant personality. Whether that dominant voice is generally a force for good or for evil, you might get used to not making decisions, or at least to adapting yourself to the decisions of that dominant person around you. When you are in the orbit of someone with outsized gravitational pull, sometimes it is hard to get your own sense of personal stability.

Decision anxiety fits naturally here, complicating even mundane decisions. For example, you look at a restaurant menu and wonder what other people would think is a good choice, not what *you* want to eat. You've come to find a measure of security only when someone you trust can assure you that you are making the right choice.

Perhaps one or more of these examples didn't require much imagination from you because you grew up accustomed to seeing your choices primarily through the eyes of others, or you often felt the need to defer to others rather than gradually making more decisions. If this is you, you may find it helpful to scan back through your family life. It can be helpful to consider where it was that you might have picked up the idea that the feelings of people around you needed to be taken care of, watched out for carefully, or babysat. Consider asking, "What am I afraid will happen if I disappoint others?"

Facing these fears is important, but it's wise to do this prayerfully, with a trusted friend or counselor. It doesn't need to be an archaeological dig through the past; it's a nonjudgmental reflection of how you tend to navigate the world because often that mode of navigating (hiding, placating, avoiding conflict, etc.) is something you learned or at least have practiced for reasons that made sense at the time. It may have been a useful way to engage your circumstances or mitigate dangers in the past, but the circumstances have now changed, and your reliance on these old responses is getting you stuck in the mire of decision anxiety.

This feeling of getting stuck in our anxieties fits well with Proverbs 29:25: "Fearing people is a dangerous trap, but trusting the LORD means safety" (NLT). Fear of others gets us caught, tied up, and trapped when we make our decisions because we are overfocused on avoiding complications, conflicts, criticism, and negative consequences. Fearing others' reactions or opinions can take over our lives if we let it. We learn these fears early and often—they are well reinforced. But they can be unlearned—we can come to a place of safety by trusting the Lord.

Life is complicated, and everything is not our parents' fault. It's important to point out that often one sibling will grow up responding to family difficulty by becoming highly anxious, and another sibling within the same family will respond to the difficulty by deciding that it's impossible to please people, so why try? There will always be some mystery, some degree of the unknown, when we try to understand problems like decision anxiety. But we can see patterns. Some people seem to be temperamentally anxious, or they tend toward obsessiveness from an early age. Sometimes there appears to be no real discernible source for the anxiety. But we all learn something about what we should value and protect, and what we should be afraid of from our families. We learn what kinds of risks we should fear the most and how we should navigate those risks. Uncovering these influences, especially the less helpful messages about what we should fear and how we should seek safety, can help us answer them with truth. Here are a few brief examples of how the messages we hear from our families can be answered with the truth:

Learned Message (implicit or explicit)	Biblical Response
You need to come across as well put together and confident, or things will not go well for you.	God often uses what the world sees as weakness to do great things, and Jesus himself came in humility.
You're always screwing things up. What is wrong with you?	All my efforts are imperfect, but I'm a saint and a child of God, a work in progress who is dearly loved. God loves to be patient with me.
If it's worth doing, it's worth doing well, and it's worth doing it right the first time. Someone else would do a better job.	God has called me here in this time and place to be a friend/mom/husband/worker. He will give me what I need not so I can be better than everyone else, but so I can be faithful.

There are at least as many possible fears as there are families, so you might have many examples come to mind as you reflect on the past. Often you will find that the opposite of what your family values is what your family fears. The families that highly value education will typically fear academic failure or mediocrity. Those that value timeliness, cleanliness, thinness, or general excellence will typically fear perceived failure or mediocrity in these areas as well. No family will be totally devoid of all wise values or concerns, and no family will perfectly balance the many possible biblical values and concerns. The goal is not to condemn or exonerate but to learn and grow.

To reflect on family is to step onto sensitive ground. Ask someone what it was really like to grow up in their household, and you will quickly see you've entered quite an intimate place, whether the feelings that arise are gratitude or grief. Family matters profoundly. And yet it is also relativized by Jesus in ways that make us more loving and loyal family members on the one hand and constructive disrupters of family systems on the other. Jesus condemns legalistic approaches to the law that lead to people not taking care of their family members (Matthew 15:3–6), and he also teaches that the family of God is our profound ultimate connection—it is those who do God's will that he counts as his family (Matthew 12:46–50). Jesus calls us to a place of courageous love, continuing as those who honor father and mother even at personal sacrifice, and also being willing to break some traditions that failed the test of loving others and trusting God.

For some of us, the burden of some traditions and spoken and unspoken rules in the family has been heavy. It has led to anxiety in dating, for example, because you find yourself asking whether your family was right to fear marrying someone with a more checkered past. Or you struggle with whether taking on school debt is truly something to fear on the level you were taught, or whether it would be wise in your case for the short term. Some decisions carry anxieties directly shaped by our families.

We should be clear on our expectations: deciding to break family rules will heighten anxiety in the short term. So although being oriented to biblical wisdom will sometimes lead to conflict with our families, we will always want to take these hard steps humbly and in community, with spiritually mature brothers and sisters walking with us. Jesus sometimes calls us toward conflict with family, but he never wants us to walk alone (Mark 10:29–30). This orientation toward constructive relationships with others and primary loyalty to God will serve as a necessary foundation for each of the areas we'll survey in part 3. As we look at marriage, vocation, and smaller decisions, we'll consider ways that God offers us his presence and wisdom to more faithfully engage our world.

QUESTIONS FOR REFLECTION

1. What are some family traditions or rules that you have really appreciated? What are some that you have come into conflict with?

2. What are some family messages or values that still give you confidence? What are messages or values that you suspect have contributed to your anxiety?

3. God calls us to love our families loyally and sacrificially but also to sometimes engage in conflict for the family's good. In what ways is God inviting you to grow in both?

PART 3:
HOW TO CHANGE

Chapter 6

ANXIETY ABOUT MARRIAGE: HOW KNOWING GOD AND KNOWING YOURSELF BRINGS CLARITY

"Is it really your anxiety that stops you from giving me everything?" — "Renegade," Big Red Machine[1]

Deciding to marry someone is one of the most difficult arenas of decision anxiety because we know marriage is consequential. On the one hand, we treat decision anxiety as a problem in relationships because it's possible that anxiety is overinflating concerns that may be relatively insignificant. We don't want to be paralyzed by the kind of anxiety that keeps us from something really good. On the other hand, anxiety about marriage feels warranted. We ultimately know that this kind of anxiety may be on to something. Maybe this person isn't a great fit. Maybe we will overlook a big problem. Maybe we will have regrets. The difficult truth is that Christians who approach the decision prayerfully, humbly, and in community sometimes still walk into very hard marriages. This is truly sobering.

We can't convince ourselves that the decision is inconsequential. By comparison, making a difficult job-related decision may be a big fork in the road and highly consequential, but it's not lifelong. It doesn't make children, a family, or a home. So anxiety latches onto this and doesn't let go easily. Everyone wants to avoid bad outcomes in dating, so some degree of anxiety and apprehensiveness is to be expected. But when these fears are more intense, they make it hard to stay in the present and take things one step, one date at a time.

It's also hard to stay in the present and let things develop naturally because anxiety tends to get us stuck on evaluating our feelings. And we usually decide whether to go forward in a relationship partly *based* on how it feels. I don't say this as a criticism but as a statement of reality. Of course, feelings alone are not the foundation of a good relationship. If you are dating someone, and the basic, foundational criteria (shared faith, good character, some capacity to collaborate, a modicum of ability to navigate conflict in a productive way, etc.) are there, then deciding to get married comes down to whether you want to go forward, whether you desire this relationship, and whether you believe it is a good and wise thing. Our feelings of desire, confidence, and peace are always part of the equation within a culture of unarranged, companionate marriages. So, what do you do when you feel anxious about whether you should continue moving forward in a relationship?

You know what this feels like. First, the pang of nervousness comes with a perceived risk or just a vague uneasiness, and then the presence of anxiety itself becomes a threat. *If I'm so uncertain, does that mean I shouldn't move forward?* Then ruminating and self-loathing can come in. *What's wrong with me? This is a good person; why am I struggling to move forward?* Anxiety and self-loathing are a powerful one-two punch. We know anxiety can hijack lots of good things in life, so it can feel exasperating to see it getting in the way of a relationship that really could be a good thing.

Sometimes the sense of risk steals whatever confidence, excitement, and hope we had in starting the relationship.

COUNTERINTUITIVE WISDOM: LISTEN TO YOUR ANXIETY

In one sense, the problem with anxiety is that it overinflates the sense of risk, and we respond with ineffective efforts to get rid of the risk. So we want to live as those who trust the Lord right through the dangers and not let risk avoidance dictate our actions. And yet as we saw in chapter 1, when the alarm bell of anxiety goes off, we do have to make sure there isn't a fire burning somewhere. Anxiety can be an indicator that something is wrong, so we have to engage in discernment when anxiety signals the presence of a serious risk.

This sense of risk is hardest when it is vague rather than focused on a specific relational dynamic or character problem in the other person. Sometimes people feel extremely nervous about deciding to marry the person they're dating, and they don't really know why; they just feel really scared. From a marriage counselor's perspective, it is difficult not to step in here to say that often, when anxiety is high within a dating relationship, the anxiety is pointing at real risks that probably need to be resolved before moving forward with marriage. The hesitation in making this a general rule is that some people realize over time they are not afraid of the relationship they're in but rather of marriage and commitment in general. For example, someone might be confident the person they are dating is not an alcoholic, but their childhood experience with one—and seeing its effects on family—has left them nervous about where a relationship that at first seemed good can go wrong. Other times the anxiety resolves itself as you give the relationship time and connection and trust build.

Sometimes, when this vague anxiety persists, our brains are recognizing a pattern of concerning relationship dynamics before we can put those concerns into words. We only feel uneasy. Maybe you have not seen the person you're dating actually become intensely angry or violent, but some of his behavior leaves you uncomfortable or unsettled in ways you can't put into words. You don't yet have the clarity that you may later have to say you feel indirectly blamed or subtly pressured by this person much of the time; right now you just feel confused and anxious.[2] This is partly how intuition works. Sometimes we feel that something is not right, but we can't yet explain why. And sometimes, because the discomfort is vague, people who are less secure or confident in their judgment will discount their own concerns.

Here it can be important to take some time to slow down and reflect on your concerns, to see if you can locate specific sources of the distress. Sometimes you'll find that anxiety does focus on something—fear of how your differences will play out in parenting, fear of the chemistry not being great and that will make marriage harder, or fear of how the person's current behaviors will affect the marriage (e.g., overdrinking, overspending, maintaining friendships with former girlfriends or boyfriends). Or what if your family isn't really on board with the person you're dating? What if your values aren't as aligned as you thought at first? What if you see a significant, unaddressed character flaw? The presence of any of these will bring some degree of anxiety. And in these examples, anxiety will likely persist and build unless there is some resolution.

The advice not to marry in hopes of changing someone is one instance of popular advice being on target. It's wise to ask, Is this person, as the person is now, someone whom I could see being a good spouse and parent

with me? For certain problems, a long period of absti-
nence from the addictive practices (e.g., alcohol, hookups,
gambling, etc.) needs to be there, along with proactive
confessions and disclosures. As a general rule, addictive
patterns that only stopped recently, or are still happening,
are likely to continue. A common rule of thumb for alcohol abuse, for example, is to complete a year of sobriety
before dating. With any problem, deception should be a
red flag—the red should be bright and the flag should
be big. God certainly can change people, and all people
have a past that includes sin and shame. Even so, the best
predictor of who the person will be is who the person has
consistently been over time.

As my cautions above should indicate, anxiety about
a relationship can emerge for important reasons. Anxiety
points to risks. Figuring out what to do with the risks you
find in your relationship is the priority here. Anxiety tar-
gets risk and sets off the alarm for you to do something
with it. That action step is often a breakup when anxiety
about whether to move forward in a relationship becomes
severe. As a couple, you conclude that if one of you is not
confident enough in moving forward, you don't want to
stay together. But what if you do stay in the relationship
when anxiety is high? You have to figure out what to do
with the risks or how to make sense of the risks.

It's this struggle of confidence that I want to focus
on. Not every Christian struggles in this way. Some are
too confident, sure of themselves, and decisive. They may
consult a book on decisions, but probably not on decision
anxiety, because they usually need to slow down, exercise
more caution, listen to more people, and engage in a process of discernment that runs counter to their natural way
of making decisions.

But for people struggling with decision anxiety, there is a deficit of steadiness or confidence in their decisions. This can affect every stage of the decision process and comes up in questions such as these:

- Am I being too picky, or should I give this person a first or second date?
- I'm not that attracted to this person, but should I give it more time just in case?
- I see some problems, but I know I'm not perfect either, so maybe I should give it more time to see if the person changes?
- I'm not sure that we're a great fit, but opposites attract, right?

You can hear in each one of the questions a sense of unsteadiness and hesitation.

So how do you get to a place of steadiness and find the ability to move forward? Many of these questions can be resolved when given adequate time. As you spend more time with the person, either the connection and excitement build so that you strongly want to move forward, or clarity and confidence lead to an honest conversation. I am interested in helping you cultivate the skills of knowing what it is you want to do and growing in confidence to take action in light of what you know. Knowing who you are, how God made you, makes it much easier to decide who fits well with you as a spouse.

KNOW YOURSELF

I wonder if this sounds like the tired narrative of self-discovery. I'm talking about the story line at the center of so many movies and popular songs—the independent quest to find the deepest and truest self within and then to accept and express it. Christians believe that this narrative doesn't capture the full story, that it misses a key paradox of the Christian life—in following Jesus, we deny ourselves, die to ourselves, and give it all up; and yet, we also *find ourselves* in the story of God's redemption (Matthew 16:24–25). We become more who we were destined to be in the creation plan. We are not only discovered and affirmed (though thankfully we are!), but we're also restored then continually refined and transformed. The self we "find" is the self we're becoming, one with the happy calling of being trained in love and Christian virtue in community, rather than a self that is primarily uncovered by looking within.

To say we need accurate self-knowledge isn't just buying into self-focused messages from our culture. Knowing ourselves is important for Christian reasons. An early Christian by the name of Gregory said that not knowing who we are is the main reason we struggle with indecisiveness. "They disregard and undervalue themselves too greatly," he says. "If they would at all consider what they are, the wind of mutability would not turn them in so many directions."[3]

Gregory draws from several biblical texts to argue that indecisive people struggle and feel unsteady because they are like a building without a solid foundation. He says they lack an underlying firmness, a sobriety or weightiness, and so they get tossed around (Ephesians 4:14) and end up stuck on both a yes and a no (2 Corinthians 1:17). Gregory explains from Ephesians that the opposite of this instability is to be like a child who grows into maturity, which means growing up into Christlikeness (Ephesians 4:13). As this growth occurs, Gregory says, then our yes and no are firmer (Matthew 5:37).[4] Maturity, or spiritual adulthood, brings consistency and opinions, preferences and goals, direction and decisiveness—all out of a conscious sense of gifting and calling. Ephesians 4 gives us a picture of maturing faith that brings *voice*.[5]

As you have a better sense of your goals and dreams in life, you have a better sense of who would be a good fit to pursue those with you—and whose goals and dreams you'd like to sign on to as well. You'll both always need to be flexible and willing to be refined by each other's differences, but it's good to start with mostly shared big goals. It really helps to discover what makes you tick.

Pursuing accurate self-knowledge is an important part of deciding what kind of person matches well with you. It also helps you better know whether the relationship you are in now is a good fit and gives you greater confidence in evaluating the relationship. It is worth the effort. That said, knowing yourself well isn't an obsessive archaeological dig or a long and solitary journey of self-exploration. The theologian John Calvin starts his *Institutes* by saying that knowing God and knowing yourself are connected. As you look inward, you naturally look upward, and as you look upward, you naturally look back inward. There's an interplay. Of course, there is more to maturing into adulthood than spiritual maturity. But the rootedness and solidity that comes from a steady relationship with God are vitally important for staying steady through the confusion that can come with decision anxiety in dating. This does not mean that confusion and unsteadiness are necessarily unspiritual, only that maturing spiritually grows in us a sense of abiding steadiness as we build our house on the rock and increasingly feel, as the song says, "all other ground is sinking sand."

PRAY FOR WHAT YOU WANT

One way to grow up into this steadiness or sturdiness as a Christian is to start at the beginning, to pray like a child and, specifically, to ask for things. People struggling with decision anxiety in a relationship often feel they can't trust themselves or that they don't know what they want. Part of growing up is having a sense of agency, a level of acceptance that you are a person who desires and thinks and then acts, who walks with God and longs to see his kingdom come and will be done, that more of heaven would come down to earth in your corner of the world. Prayers of petition mean we look at our world and reflect on what we want to see God doing. And in relationship with God, those wants are shaped further to reflect his heart of love for our little world, our work, and our relationships. The more we know him, and the more we learn about his heart in the Bible, the more we understand the kinds of prayers he loves to say yes to. "This is the confidence we have in approaching God: that if we ask anything according to his will, he hears us" (1 John 5:14).

Prayers of petition are practice in how to want things—whether that is a job change, a ministry opportunity, or a life companion. This kind of prayer leads to spiritually mature action. Over time, you see connections between what you are praying for and how God is opening doors, which will help you take constructive action in that direction. How often does he answer our prayers for opportunities to share the gospel, for example, by sending the most unexpected conversations our way? So I encourage starting to get in the habit of thinking about what you want and asking for it. What kind of friend do you wish you could be? What kind of relationship would you like to have with your neighbors? What opportunities to serve resonate with you, what needs do you notice, and what suffering do you see around you? How would you desire to see God act? These kinds of prayers can move mountains, and they are part of a childlike relationship with your Father, but they also bring clarity to you as you pray. You develop a vision for your life and your world by this kind of prayer.

Having vision and pursuing it is part of maturity. When we know better how we fit in this world and how we want to navigate this life, we will create connections with others who want these same things. This is helpful for every believer, both those who marry and those who remain single. As we engage the process of faithfully navigating God's world and seeking to exercise our spiritual gifts in particular ways, we find spiritual companions for the journey. Knowing your desired place and areas of service in this world—knowing where you want to go—will make it easier to decide whether a particular person is a good fit as a companion on this journey, or whether you would be a good fit for that person. It's not about definitively nailing down your place in the world and your opportunities of service in the kingdom. Our calling can change over the seasons of life, and we change too. We don't have to reach the full conclusion to benefit from the process—and we won't in this life. But because most decision anxiety about dating is connected to the question of whether we're a good fit, engaging this process of understanding ourselves and our place in the world works directly against decision anxiety. We're better at deciding whether a relationship is a good fit as we learn about the potential puzzle pieces, starting with us. And in the process, we also learn who God is and become those who praise him more and more, honoring him as the source of the wisdom we're seeking and of every good thing (James 1:5, 17).

If focusing, in seasons, on asking God for what you want sounds selfish to you, consider what Paul Miller says in *A Praying Life*: sometimes we believers can get too "spiritual" for our own good, that we can so quickly accept a posture of surrender that we don't experience ourselves as having wants and hurts. This is especially true of many anxious people I've walked with. Miller gives the example of a man who tends to "[submit] so quickly to God that he as a person can't emerge. Christians rush to 'not my will but yours be done' without first expressing their hearts (Luke 22:42). They submit so quickly they disappear." He continues, "When we stop being ourselves with God, we are no longer in real conversation with God."[6] Rather than being selfish, the right kind of self-knowledge and prayerful expression is part of a real relationship with God.

Reflexive, immediate self-abnegation prevents you from speaking your heart to your Father in heaven and enjoying fellowship with him. But being a person—a Christian person—means utilizing the capabilities God built you with. He made you to feel things, to want things, to ask for things. Yes, our feelings and desires are fallen. But we were created with the capacity for feelings and desires—and when God recreates us, he redeems what is fallen rather than erasing it.

It is not easy to bring yourself to him as you are because, of course, we know that all the things we want to be can feel far from who we are right now. Yet to have a real relationship with God is to relate to him as you really are, not as you wish to be or hope to be. And if we don't know what we lack, we won't know what to ask for. If one aspect of what it means to pray is to verbalize a want, then praying requires a willingness to want things and to voice a request. This is because personhood involves agency, preferences, and desires. Prayers of petition disrupt a reactionary mode of life and invite proactivity. And this kind of initiative is part of what it means to live as an adult.

That all may sound great in theory. But what if, right now, you're nervous and starting to feel paralyzed? Setting a basic goal of identifying the sources of the anxiety and seeing how each one can be resolved is a good start. When you are struggling to find resolution, facing the fears directly is best. Be willing to admit what you see and what raises your concern. The following paragraphs give a few examples of how prayers lead to clarity and can help you resolve specific anxieties. Most anxieties about relationships fall into these three categories.

1. *Compatibility.* Start with honesty. What do you see? Perhaps you see differences that bother you and make collaboration difficult (views on work–life balance, the value of education, parenting approaches, political or class-based differences). In prayer, clarify what you want. Example: "I want to see us being able to work together well on most things, to give and serve each other mutually, to compromise and find solutions, and to love and honor one another in areas where we tend to navigate life differently. I want to see us both loving grace, and specifically repairing well when we hurt each other, and practicing humble repentance and forgiveness." This kind of prayer leads to clarity in what qualities you want to see over time, and it will not usually require a long period of time to know whether this kind of relationship is developing.

2. *Character.* Identify the source of the character concern. Does the person frequently spend in a highly impulsive way, get into consumer debt, and then regret it? Or how frequent is the pornography struggle occurring, and how proactive is the person in humbly seeking help and change? How does the person respond when you express concern about the level of drinking? Perhaps most importantly, does the person respond to feedback with humility, honesty, and restorative action? In prayer, clarify what you are asking for. Example: I want to see evidence that the problem has been addressed or is being addressed. I want to see this person confessing proactively to others and to me if the problem

resurfaces. I want to see this person respond with grace and without defensiveness or blame-shifting when I share my concerns about this issue. I want to have the courage to leave if needed. This kind of prayer brings both clarity and also courage to act in light of the clarity that emerges over time.

3. *Connection.* Is the sense of connection in the relationship building mutually? When it is not, anxiety will almost certainly be present. Sometimes admitting the source of anxiety brings resolution quickly. In this case, facing the reality that you don't truly desire a relationship with the person is a painful but clarifying admission that typically leads to a decision. But other times, the answer will not be as obvious. So try to discover something you can say that captures the concern. For example, maybe the chemistry and attraction are there but not in the way you expected. Or the chemistry and attraction are not there, but you respect and admire the person so much that you don't want to give up on the possibility. In prayer, push the fear into a request. Example: I want to see us enjoying time together, missing one another when we are apart. I want to be patient toward the process. I want to see us both wanting to go forward. This kind of prayer helps in the short term by inviting openness and patience, but it also nurtures a care for the other person that does not unnecessarily prolong a stagnant relationship.

These prayers are not simply for personal growth. For each one, it will be important to take a next step from clarifying wants and to invite God to shape our wants and values according to his love. We also want to grow in connection to God in the process, so we name the things we're asking for as either things he has promised (e.g., when we ask for patience) or things we entrust to him as requests that we are not promised (e.g., feelings of connection or chemistry in the relationship). We then praise him as the giver of every good gift (James 1:17), and as the one who walks with us through the times that call for endurance, as we wait for clarity.

SIGNS OF UNRESOLVED ANXIETY IN A RELATIONSHIP

Waiting for clarity is really difficult. We should be honest, too, that sometimes even when we take steps to know ourselves and how we fit in the world, and even when we take the steps we know of to pursue a mature steadiness and ask God for clarity, some degree of confusion remains. If you don't find resolution for the anxiety you have about your relationship, then it becomes easy to fall into one (or more) of four negative relationship patterns. If any of these descriptions sound true of you and your relationship, take note of the suggestions I provide for the kinds of changes and hard decisions you might need to make.

1. Holding On in a Relationship

Decision anxiety often leads to delayed breakups, which in the end sadly leads to more hurt for both people. Sometimes this takes the form of trying to save someone or longing to be the one who can change the person or call forth the best in that person. The tragic reality is that the work of being a messiah is much too big for any one of us. This requires us to face painful and sobering realities, and many find them to be some of the most difficult and confusing situations to leave. Related, sometimes the fear of no better option can keep us feeling trapped in a relationship that really is not a good fit. Here it is important to remember what many have lived, and what Deepak Reju says well: "A bad marriage is not better than struggling through singleness."[7]

2. Holding Back in a Relationship

Anxiety in a relationship that leads us to hold back can come from the feeling that a relationship is moving too fast, and that feeling is not necessarily an immediate problem. It's okay to feel nervous then to act on it by taking things more slowly. The challenge is when anxiety locks the relationship up entirely. Sometimes this anxiety comes from the fear that a better option may be out there. This is a difficult fear to face—what if a person out there is a better fit? There's no way to disprove it. It's not a romantic thing to say, but for someone who is seriously anxious, facing that possibility and entrusting even this to God is an important step forward. Related, you'll generally make the best decision when you're evaluating a relationship on its own merits and not in view of hypothetical other options.

3. Urgency toward a Potential Relationship

The fear of singleness and the fear of being alone can add pressure and anxiety to a relationship. It can also rush commitment and lead us to overlook concerns, which heightens anxiety. When we're overlooking things that we shouldn't, anxiety again is the helpful alarm bell. Here the fears are competing. On the one side, the risk of overlooking problems in the relationship stirs anxiety, and on the other, the fear of singleness is formidable. Before and even during dating, it's important to be willing to do the painful work of facing the fear and grief of potential undesired singleness. I've observed a steadiness in people who've faced this possibility and to some degree accepted it, even if it remains something they definitely do not want.

Here and in all the patterns listed, sexual activity in dating tends to make this anxiety worse. When our actions on the outside don't match what we are feeling on the inside, or when our confidence in the relationship doesn't match the physical and emotional stage of the relationship, we're likely to feel distress, confusion, and anxiety.[8]

4. Hesitancy toward a Potential Relationship

The fear of starting a relationship can lead people to get stuck in a long season of being "just friends," keeping close contact or even going on dates but never making it to commitment. The risk aversion is understandable, but ultimately it is not loving. It can be awkward or embarrassing to make the first move to discuss the relationship, and it may not go well! Even so, it's a way to communicate that the person is worth the risk, and it's a way to demonstrate a kind of love for others that takes the initiative in relationship-stage-appropriate vulnerability. And that pattern is good for a marriage—the willingness to start conversations that are vulnerable and loving builds trust and intimacy in every way.[9]

CONCLUSION

Each of these patterns of anxiety will be best addressed in a rhythm of time with the person you're dating (or potentially dating), time with friends and mentors, and time alone with God and your thoughts. Sometimes spending lots of time with the person will give you assurance to move forward—or clarify that this is not a good fit. Sometimes you'll notice lots of people you respect are speaking up about red flags. Other times friends will provide validation that eases your anxieties. Sometimes time alone with God and your thoughts brings a clarity you wouldn't otherwise have if you spent all of your free time with the person you're dating. Creating some room for mental space, reflection, and prayer is really important. It's not surprising, then, that some who study decision-making speak of the value of taking a walk, letting your mind wander, and letting your brain sort things out without an agenda or task list. It seems that our bodies and minds are made in such a way that we sometimes find our best progress in making work and life decisions by taking breaks, little Sabbaths along the way.

Decision anxiety about a relationship is like other anxieties in many key ways: it's hard to tolerate ambiguity, it's hard to live with risk, it's hard to stay present and not get stuck ruminating. It's also different in that it's harder to argue against the feeling of ultimacy or major significance. Marriage is consequential.

But the other side of the coin is that a conversation or a date is not marriage. Expressing interest is not marriage. Dating is not marriage. We don't want to be flippant with people's feelings, but we do want to relax enough to have fun and get to know people. It really can be taken one step at a time. And the individual steps we take are not usually of that much significance. Some of it really is ordinary, and that's a good thing. We don't need every step to be perfect. We want to walk in a generally faithful direction, following the Good Shepherd, "the pioneer and perfecter of our faith" (Hebrews 12:2).

QUESTIONS FOR REFLECTION

1. Do you find it difficult to know your own preferences and wants? Where does this tend to show up?

2. How might your prayers sound if you knew God welcomed your requests? What would you ask for?

3. Where do you see opportunities to take steps of love and faith in the arena of relationships?

Chapter 7

ANXIETY ABOUT VOCATION: WORKING TOWARD FAITHFUL STEWARDSHIP AND PEACE

"Had vocational counselors interviewed Simon Peter
. . . they would hardly have recommended a career
in sectarian religious extremism, as a follower of the
Nazarene. Devotion to such a cause could, and did,
end in crucifixion." — Ed Clowney[1]

The core message of the previous chapter on marriage remains applicable for vocation. It is difficult to know what kind of vocation is a good fit if we do not know ourselves well, which includes knowing our interests, preferences, hopes, commitments, relationships, and much more. Knowing ourselves accurately, as Christians, involves knowing God and living in Christian community, and a special help is available to us as we work toward spiritual maturity. The help is the practice of praying, of asking for things like a child. Prayer strengthens us, helps us know our place in the world, and connects us to our bigger, orienting spiritual values. It brings us close to the heart of God and shapes and refines our loves and wants. Prayers of petition, in themselves, force us to clarify what it is we want because we are explicitly asking.

For example, when I stop and consider where I most want to see God's kingdom come and will be done, it clarifies the concerns that most burden me. If I were to find myself especially burdened about children in the foster care system, my prayers will likely strengthen this burden and generate further reflection on how I can help. Ideas of respite care, fostering, supporting families in other ways, or even considering working full time in social services will naturally arise. We don't know what God will do with our burdens, but he will nurture godly ambitions and typically bring them to some form of action. I've also often found that praying for opportunities to serve others and share the love of Jesus orients me toward others and makes me more ready when the opportunities come.

This is true, too, of vocations that are less straight-forwardly service oriented. In Martin Luther's words, "When a prince sees his neighbor oppressed, he should think: That concerns me! I must protect and shield my neighbor." He continues, "The same is true for shoemaker, tailor, scribe, or reader. If he is a Christian tailor, he will say: I make these clothes because God has bidden me do so, so that I can earn a living, so that I can help and serve my neighbor."[2] Wherever we work, we look for how we might take faithful steps forward to work against what destroys God's good creation and to work for what brings God's kingdom and peace. Shane Claiborne makes similar points frequently. Not everyone needs to leave their careers to serve in the most underserved neighborhoods or overseas. But, in his words, "When we truly encounter Jesus and the poor, we may still be a tax collector, but we will be a different kind of tax collector. We may still be a doctor, but we will be a different kind of doctor."[3]

In addition to providing avenues for service, we glorify God by simply doing work, just as we were created to, as those who order, arrange, and tend to the world like Adam and Eve.[4] The often-quoted words of Olympian Eric Liddell saying he felt God's pleasure when he was running hold true. Doing what we're good at and enjoying it is a beautiful thing. To that end, knowing our preferences and our proclivities is a good start. I probably wouldn't make a good chemist, accountant, or mechanic, but we absolutely need people who would. So we do need to consider what it is we want to do and whether we (and others) think we might do a decent job at it. Prayer, practice, relationships, and reflection over time clarify these things for us.

Prayer in particular connects us to God and each other. When we pray, we grow closer in our experience of relationship with God. With other believers, there is almost nothing like prayer that connects us as deeply, that engages us so intimately and personally. Some of the basic criteria for how friendship happens are "proximity; repeated, unplanned interactions; and a setting that encourages people to let their guard down and confide in each other."[5] Times of prayer with friends can do all three. Friendship with Jesus, the friend of sinners, is similar. Time spent with God that is regular, spontaneous, and honest strengthens the relationship with him too. And close relationship, with God and with others, works directly against anxiety. We are less afraid when we are less alone. Anxiety thrives in isolation. That is true of decisions related to dating and marriage and true of decisions about where we work and live. To grow as decision-makers, we pursue identity formation and Christian maturity through prayer in community.

The main addition that this chapter provides is that we must learn to be faithful stewards of the little corner of creation that God has invited us to cultivate. Knowing what job is a good fit for us requires us to go a step further than interests and talents. So vocation—calling—is not primarily something found inside us. It suggests that someone is doing the calling—there is a voice; there are words for us from outside of us. As Amy Sherman says, "Discipling for vocational stewardship involves not only the work of inspiration and discovery but also an emphasis on formation."[6] We're part of something bigger and richer than finding our ideal individual life. We want to faithfully manage the gift of God's good creation with hearts shaped by God's ideal for life and work in a worshipping community: *shalom*. This is what we were made for: "an expression and extension" not of ourselves, but the peace of God because we are working as ministers of reconciliation (2 Corinthians 5:18).[7]

WHY IS STEWARDSHIP SO HARD?

Let's start with what makes it so difficult to serve as stewards or managers of creation. Part of the challenge comes with the fact that our decisions can feel ultimate, especially about our careers. And we have to face the fact that they are consequential. But if decisions are an arena for our formation and discipleship, then they provide us opportunities to be faithful and grow today. Our decisions are never perfect, but we become better managers of life over time, especially as we know more of the heart of God.

Another part of the challenge is the unique pressure on work in a modern context. Henry Ford said it more explicitly than most of us, but there is a cultural pressure that transforms work into "our sanity, our self-respect, our salvation."[8] This sentiment is not completely unique to modern times. Work has always been significant. My ancestors' surname before an adoption in Sicily was *Vaca*—cow. Their name told how they worked for a living—raising cows. It's the same with most of my other ancestors—the Smiths, Taylors, Millers, and Saccomannos. What we do and where we live tell us something about who we are as persons—they *name* us even still. That's not new. But what is newer is that, in the United States majority culture, these things are largely all our choice. It was in no way expected or certain that I would do for a living what my dad did, nor that I'd stay in South Carolina. For me, as with my parents, pursuing the career I wanted (or education in that direction) required leaving home. If learning who we are helps us make big decisions in life, then it is important to recognize that what is required of many young adults in the United States is to move away from traditional sources of identity. During our crucial decision-making years, we are farther than ever from the people who could tell us who we are and where we fit in the world. Mobility has provided opportunity, but it has broken up our deep community roots and connections. The individual burden to self-explore and self-create in the arena of vocation is significant.[9]

Another complication is that Christians often look for a special calling from God to decide on a career. The sense that all work is spiritual, not only ministerial jobs, is a gift to us from the Reformation. We can truly offer up our work to serve God and neighbor. But in the normal course of events, God gives us what we need to make a decision rather than stepping in to make our decisions for us. He offers guidance, care, and even his presence with us, and then he invites us to step into our calling as managers of what belongs to him—stewardship of our little corner of the world.

You may already act as an empowered manager in other areas. Maybe you are not worried about what God thinks you should order off the Chipotle menu (though this subject is part of the next chapter). You live with a basic confidence that God has entrusted that decision to you. Sometimes it's easier to believe God has given us authority to decide small tasks, but we need to hear from him directly about the bigger tasks, like vocation. It's easy to feel like those bigger decisions belong in a different category—a category not of our decision-making but of finding his will. Of course we should be oriented to God's will for us, and he promises to provide us everything necessary for life and godliness (2 Peter 1:3). But we typically won't know for sure whether God is telling us to take one job over another. Here is how this works. God gives us what we need to love others and walk with him today, and so we are grateful. God does not remove all uncertainty and ambiguity in life, and so we are dependent. God loves and leads us in both dark valleys and green pastures, and so we are hopeful.

Most of the time we have only a lamp for our feet and a light a few feet in front of us on our path (Psalm 119:105). How I've often wished it were a floodlight! But it is a lamp—life saving and constantly helpful, but it is a lamp, and the world can feel quite dark. In this life, what we know is partial and incomplete, and this can be unsettling. How can we not worry about tomorrow (Matthew 6:34)? If we cannot reliably access God's specific, secret will for our next job—if we have light only for the immediate path in front of us, and clarity for today and not tomorrow, what should we be oriented toward?

STEWARDSHIP CULTIVATES *SHALOM* INSIDE AND OUTSIDE US

To be faithful stewards of the time, talents, and resources God has given us, we need to be oriented to the peace of God. By this I mean the rich biblical sense of *shalom*, of peace, prosperity, welfare, and wholeness. Certainly, inner peacefulness is a counterpoint or answer to decision anxiety. That's part of it. We long for the day when our fears and tears are finally wiped away, and when no rebellion and hatefulness are left in us, and we're fully at peace. Peace within involves hating wars of every kind, both inside of us and outside of us. While in this life we will always face the inner conflict between the Spirit and the flesh (Galatians 5:17), we long to see the Spirit winning more and more, and we long to experience more and more of the peace he brings, which surpasses all understanding (Philippians 4:7). And this growing peace within naturally fosters a desire for peace outside us. As peacemakers and ministers of reconciliation, we cannot make peace outside when there is no peace inside.[10] So our work to seek God's peace within us, however imperfectly, equips us to seek God's peace in our world. The person characterized by the fruit of the Spirit has a steadiness and focus: strength is disciplined into meekness, urgency and passion are bridled by patience and gentleness, compassion and concern do not overtake a deep and abiding joy.

And our peace or lack of peace is never isolated to ourselves. Who we are and how we live have an impact. Our decisions have consequences on other people. The biblical conception of peace is deeper than the individual's feeling of peacefulness. It's possible to feel or profess peace when there is no peace (Jeremiah 8:11). Real peace, the *shalom* of God, is the sense that things are arranged in the right way and ordered so that it's good for everyone. As one writer says, *shalom* is "where nothing is missing and nothing is broken."[11] Our desire to look for and help those who are lost and suffering, wandering and hurting, will always complicate our individual dreams and plans, breaking them down then reforming them to include a deep desire to do good (Galatians 6:10; Ephesians 2:10).

Being a good Samaritan means we don't get from Jeru-salem to Jericho as quickly or efficiently, and our plans become complicated by God's invitation to a costly love. But what a wonderful "complication" to be redirected and slowed down, if it helps us live as those who follow the heart of God.

To be captured by a love for God and his work in the world will break down whole categories of anxiety. Achievement, wealth, and status concerns regularly stoke our anxieties. But to be driven by a whole other set of values is to take the wind out of the sails of these anxieties. The Bible also offers clear pictures of what it looks like when this trusting posture toward God is absent.

Looking for peace amid danger has always been a time of trial and temptation for God's people. In the Hebrew Scriptures, we see the persistent tendency of people to try to protect or pursue *shalom* away from God. We see in Jeremiah 2:13,

> My people have committed two sins:
> They have forsaken me,
>   the spring of living water,
> and have dug their own cisterns,
>   broken cisterns that cannot hold water.

On the one hand, we sometimes neglect the kind of help available from God. On the other, we set up protective measures that don't hold water—they just don't work.

The people of God are also tempted to try to sustain life and survive by pursuing other gods. Fear makes false refuge alluring. It can be hard for people in modern times in some contexts to feel the allure of leaving their own faith to visit the shrine of another religion. But in ancient times, the temptation was powerful. Who wouldn't want to do anything they could, any fertility ritual or sacrifice to any god if it might give a better chance of avoiding a crop failure? An idol held out the allure of protecting everything of importance or needed for survival—work, way of life, home, and identity.

Perhaps modern times change the contours but not the fact of temptation to follow the ways of the world around us. This is particularly the case with vocation. We learn what to fear and how to protect what matters to us. And we will benefit from periodically considering how to allow the truth of God to shape what matters to us rather than simply receiving this from the world around us.

The narratives of vocation commonly available to us in the majority culture of the United States are often quite less than Christian, even if they keep some of the language of calling. These incomplete or false narratives can be persuasive in the church as well. Adam Gustine gives one example of this kind of narrative or script when he says, "We have discipled people to believe that faith is nothing more than a personal relationship with God whereby I am saved, discover my individual identity, discern God's unique purpose for my life, and learn how my passions are things God gave me to, generally speaking, make the world a better place."[12] Why is this a problem? This easily leads people to misunderstand what it means to be God's people. As one writer says, this leads to church "existing to encourage individual fulfillment rather than being a crucible to engender individual conversion into the Body."[13] There is a direct impact on decision-making when our connection to God's people is weak and the flourishing of others is not in view. As Gustine says, "We come to decision-making as *individuals* concerned in the main *about personal self-interest*. This is the idol of self at work."[14] When decisions about vocation are primarily focused on finding the one thing that I, individually, should accomplish in this world, I am much more likely to be filled with anxiety than when I approach this decision with the humble question, "How can I serve the body of Christ? How can I spread God's *shalom* in the world?" We can be ministers of peace in many ways, so when our decisions about vocation are informed by these kinds of questions, we are freer to recognize that choosing any one of the many godly ways we can serve others is a good decision.

STEWARDSHIP INVOLVES COMMUNITY

The alternative is to seek discernment for tough decisions in community. Gustine invites us to ask, "What seems good to us and the Holy Spirit here?" In this vision of vocation and calling, the church engages in discerning together with a person or family. And then, rather than controlling or coercing members toward an outcome, or being outside the process entirely, the church has the joy of being involved, of praying over and encouraging people as they move on to a new job or location or of appreciating together a continuation of our shared life.

To live as a community seeking and stewarding God's *shalom*, we are freer to engage risks. As we feel strengthened by one another in difficulty, we are more resilient to the difficulties we face. Paul's epistles are full of brief and extended words of appreciation for being prayed for and taken care of through the risks he faced. So what risks can we help one another face?

The overwhelming feeling of risk is, of course, the essence of decision anxiety regarding vocation. It does make a difference which path we choose, and the questions aren't easy:

- How much school debt should I incur toward a career I'm not sure I even want?
- I know I want to go into the medical field, but I have to decide on a track soon, and I am stuck—should I be a nurse, physician assistant, or doctor?
- Is it really okay to leave traditional schooling altogether to focus on music or my trade?

For the anxious, sometimes taking strengths inventories or visiting the school's career placement office can add to, rather than answer, these questions. I'm not sure what to do with the results I got—should I become a librarian or manage a nursing home? The test results generated "actor," but how can I figure out if that is even realistic? And is that the life I want?

Seeking to be stewards of our time and talents in community may not give us clear-cut answers to these difficult questions, but the shared life of the church does offer help to mitigate the risks we face in making these decisions. Being in the church community also offers us relational support and reminders of the biblical, broad guidelines that can inform our thinking as we seek to make God-honoring decisions about our vocation.

Celebrate the Fruits of Good Decisions and Support Each Other through the Consequences of Poor Decisions

The people of God live as those who understand the principle of reaping and sowing. Much of the wisdom tradition (especially Proverbs) in the Hebrew Scriptures follows this principle of helping each other toward the path of life and away from the paths of destruction. The cycles of blessing and curse in the books of Judges and Kings demonstrate that, in general, we reap what we sow. Many of the key events in the Bible also display the principle that poor choices result in negative consequences: the fall, the flood, and the tower of Babel. And positively, the one who walks with the wise becomes wise, the humble are exalted, and those who draw near to God will find God drawing near to them. When we see our brothers and sisters in Christ reaping the good fruit of what they have sown, we rejoice with them!

There's a danger here though. When the principle of reaping what we sow (Galatians 6:7) stands on its own, it feels hopeless. It can lend itself to judgmentalism. We hear this in Luke 18:11–12, which says, "The Pharisee stood by himself and prayed: 'God, I thank you, that I am not like other people—robbers, evildoers, adulterers—or even like this tax collector. I fast twice a week and give a tenth of all I get.'" The implication is clear: "I'm doing the right things, so I am the right kind of person, and I have the blessings and reputation to show for it." Yet Jesus says this person had it wrong. Instead, it was the humble tax collector who "went home justified before God" (Luke 18:14). The Spirit of God is gracious to the undeserving; this is a central part of the gospel's message. For an Old Testament example, consider Isaiah 40. When the people have clearly strayed and fallen, the word from God is "Comfort, comfort my people" (Isaiah 40:1a). In one of Jesus's most famous parables, when the prodigal son returns humbled from the far country, the father runs to him with favor, rather than scolding (Luke 15:11–32).

While we should encourage each other to live in ways that will lead to our flourishing, we must also seek to imitate God's heart and be gracious to each other when we are suffering the consequences of our own poor decisions. We want to be people who help each other on the other end of self-inflicted painful experiences, whether we've hit rock bottom, wrecked our relationships, or sabotaged our career. Something I have seen, over and over, is that anxious people who feel connected to others are less anxious. A key part of God's plan for our growth and care is to have us in a loving, Christian community.

Help through Hardships That Follow Apparently Good Decisions

Although much of the Bible operates from the principle of sowing and reaping, a large portion of the Bible also follows the thread of innocent suffering, injustice, and paradox. Many faithful people reap what they have not sown. We see these themes in Job, Ecclesiastes, the psalms of lament, and, perhaps most poignantly, in the Suffering Servant in Isaiah, which describes Jesus and how he received suffering that he did not deserve. God's people sometimes find themselves on a wilderness journey, having to hold onto a provision of manna only for today. God's people sometimes find themselves in times of exile, far from the Promised Land and crying, "How long, O Lord?" So we help each other engage in steps of faithfulness and trust amid uncertainties of the present and amid the feelings of delayed answers to prayer.

For a brief season, I listened to a Christian radio program about financial management. The messages tended to hit a consistent note: follow this plan, with these guidelines, and it will go really well for you financially—you'll certainly be more successful than other people, so it is worth the sacrifice. People would call in for advice or to celebrate paying off debt, and some of those calls were inspiring. Then other callers called in too, but they had made poor decisions, and at times they were scolded or even mocked. They needed to sow something different to reap something different. The program tended to highlight those two kinds of stories.

But I've never forgotten one caller's story, which wasn't like the other two. It was someone who had generally been wise with money but had a physical disability that interfered with work, causing the person to come on very hard times. The financial guru's tone got a little softer, and he began to explain that the issue was not the caller's stewardship; it was "an income problem." The system of sowing and reaping, of praise or scorn, couldn't neatly incorporate suffering, especially innocent suffering. But the church must, or else we've missed the center of our faith—the innocent, suffering Savior.

Help Shape Values and Life Orientation toward the Kingdom

The Bible's wisdom is not all sowing and reaping, and it is not all innocent suffering. It's oriented not only to good or bad things in the short term for the individual. Similarly, we want to be oriented toward the community, toward God's kingdom, because wherever we live like Jesus is king, we create kingdom peace in ourselves and in our community.

The Christian message runs counter to cultural messages of seizing the day and taking the life we want by sheer force of will. It isn't what we see in fitness and diet culture, executive leadership books, or partisan cable news. We reject the pursuit of power on the world's terms. We see that the raw ambition of the disciples arguing about who was greatest gets a rebuke from Jesus, but he praises the meek, who will inherit the earth (Matthew 5:5; Luke 22:24–30). We help each other remember that our goal is not to get as much as we can for ourselves because our conviction follows the wise saying "there's enough for everyone's need but not enough for everyone's greed."

In our life together, we also have the opportunity to reject cultural messages that glorify the individual and, therefore, put pressure on individuals to be great. In contrast to popular conceptions of individualistic peace (and negotiated, give-and-take conceptions of flourishing), biblical peace is profoundly interconnected.

When Christians take communion at church, before we take the bread and wine, we're supposed to take a moment for reflection and evaluation. *Am I right with God?* And we also add, *Am I right with others?* Self-examination is really important. But the calls to "examine themselves" (1 Corinthians 11:28) and to avoid taking communion without "discerning the body of Christ" (11:29) are more than calls to personal holiness (although they're never less than this). In the early church, the *agape*, or the love feast, was a time for the church to eat together and also involved the sacred moment of taking the consecrated bread and wine. The issue was that their love feast had failed to live up to its name. The problems directly in view in the apostle Paul's letter to the Corinthian church are divisions (11:18–19) and inequities (11:20–22) among them. Some have so much food that they overeat and get drunk, while others leave still hungry. But "discerning the body of Christ" means facing where the church community really is. The problem was in how the whole thing was going and not just with individual failures. To know if we are pointed in the right direction with our Christian lives in general and our vocations in particular, we need to learn about who God is and how God has made us and called us, but this knowledge is always pursued with reference to others. Love of neighbor is intimately connected to love of God (Matthew 22:39; 1 John 4:20).

STEWARDSHIP IS FAITHFUL AND INCREMENTAL

Although this chapter has focused primarily on orienting values and the kinds of existential or spiritual reframes that I believe best help us fight anxiety, it's worth pausing for a moment to think quite practically. To be a good steward is not only to accept risk and to have our hearts in the right place, hoping the peace inside works its way out eventually in some generally fruitful way. If the owner leaves us to manage the farm, we want to learn how to do the job well for that season of stewardship.

So how do we steward vocational decisions well? We want to live in today and not focus our worries on tomorrow or our regrets on the past, so we want to take constructive action in the present. We don't want the clock to make decisions for us. So we break decisions down into more manageable chunks. You may find it helpful to utilize one of the basic templates for decision-making referenced in the resource section at the end of this book. Generally, we have to treat a decision that must be made over a season, such as what college major to select, differently than we would treat a decision that can be made in a day. We allow for a time with as many options and ideas as possible, we evaluate them in light of our goals and desires, we study and get input, we narrow options down, compile the pros and cons and assign weight to them, compare the alternatives, give time for reflection and prayer throughout, and take action. Each stage will include some anxiety, especially when we transition from one stage to the other and especially when we start cutting off options. But it will be incremental and less overwhelming than simply facing or avoiding the big decision for weeks or months.

For career or job transition decisions, you may find it helpful to use the job-fit exercise, which is a common career counseling tool with many variations. I use the most basic version more often in counseling, and it is simply a Venn diagram with one circle being the kind of work I really like doing and the other circle being what a particular job calls for. Jobs with greater overlap naturally will pique your interest, but the process is informative even when you are evaluating a job with less overlap than you'd ideally want. Sometimes you will still want to remain in (or take) that job with less overlap, but seeing the full list of the work you desire to do listed out can be generative. Perhaps you want to continue in an engineering role, but it doesn't give you an outlet to use as many of your relational or teaching skills. This opens the door to considering avocation and areas of service and ministry, and you may volunteer teaching English as a second language, tutoring in an after-school program, or helping in youth ministry. You may not have a specific goal or course of action readily in mind, but you can begin to pray for God to give opportunity to exercise those gifts that you currently have less opportunity to use in your current role. This kind of prayer and exploration can occur at any age and career stage. And career decisions can even begin to feel less ultimate when you imagine work as not the only arena for serving with the gifts God has given.

STEWARDSHIP GROWS HUMBLE TRUST

Whatever our vocation, each day we seek to mature as Christians with our calling today, and this is the best preparation for the bigger decisions tomorrow. This formation necessarily requires risk because we don't know everything we might like to know before the decision needs to be made. Another way to talk about risk is *trust*. We entrust ourselves to God when we step out and try things, when we take good risks in order to do good in the world. There's humility in this too. Because we don't know everything, we are less likely to see ourselves as masters of our fate. We really don't know how our decisions will turn out, even if today they seem like good ones. We do entrust them to our Good Shepherd, who does know the way, and who leads us even in our uncertainty and in the necessary ambiguity.

The apostle Paul reminds us, "Now I know in part; then I shall know fully, even as I am fully known" (1 Corinthians 13:12b). God knows us more than we know ourselves—and far more than we know the world around us that we are trying to make sense of. Our knowledge is partial, and this is a big part of why we are anxious. We know there is risk in what we do not know. But this gives us the opportunity to live in trust, in dependence on the good, all-knowing Father.

QUESTIONS FOR REFLECTION

1. What unhelpful values do you find yourself most tempted toward that lead to anxiety about vocation (e.g., wealth, status, achievement)?

2. In what areas of service, or what populations, do you feel concerned, grieved, inspired, or burdened to help?

3. Where do you long to see God's peace in your world? Where do you see opportunities to pursue this?

Chapter 8

ANXIETY ABOUT PLANS, PURCHASES, AND OTHER SMALL STUFF: GROWING IN SKILL AND VIRTUE

"Do the good things you're afraid of." — BJ Thompson[1]

Career, ministry, and relationships take the focus in most resources that address decision anxiety, but smaller decisions like deciding how to spend an afternoon or which purchase to make can be paralyzing too. In this chapter, we'll look at how small things can get us really stuck. We'll look at hang-ups, including the common and less common, as well as both small life interruptions and major life interruptions that come from many everyday decisions. Most of these decisions, mercifully, don't cause too much angst for most of us, but for some of us, small decisions are regularly quite difficult.

Here are a few examples of decisions that either come from anxiety or lead to it:

- Should I watch a movie or read a book tonight?
- Should I buy the store-brand or name-brand crackers? Organic bananas?

- Should I take an extra shift or be with my family this weekend?
- Should I order the buffalo chicken wrap or the southwest salad?
- Should I stay late for work if I wasn't very productive?
- Should I go back and clarify after I accidentally said something that wasn't true?

Other examples can emerge in those more plagued by obsessive and intrusive thoughts.

- Should I drive back over the route I took, just in case I might've run over something, or even someone, and not realized it?
- Should I be done reading my Bible and praying today if I haven't yet felt encouraged or close to God? If I don't feel this way, does that mean I am not sensitive to the Spirit?
- Should I attest that I read this article assigned for class if I perhaps didn't comprehend it well? Should I reread it just to be safe?

Both the everyday and the more extreme anxieties follow a similar progression. To give one snapshot, maybe you've made a joke then later worried that perhaps it was insensitive. The thought crosses your mind that maybe you should follow up with the person just in case. Then you dismiss it because it really was benign, and it would be an awkward interaction. But then you can't shake the accusatory thought, *What if I'm acting like I don't care if I hurt the person, or they think less of me because I made that comment?* Then you push back a little: *No, it probably was fine; it would be weird to bring up my own joke again—and they didn't act like it hurt them or anything.* Then anxiety circles back: *Am I just blowing off the concern? What if this feeling is my conscience flagging something I need to deal with? What does it say about me if I ignore this?* You see how anxiety compounds and intensifies. No decision feels truly safe because there is always a small possibility that you've done something wrong or unwise, and a small possibility that you're not being humble or sensitive enough to go back and fix what you've done.

If this kind of anxiety sounds foreign to you, consider it a mercy. The obsessive fears, intrusive thoughts, and immense pressure to alleviate it by any means possible are all serious afflictions. I've sat with many sincere and committed believers who explain, through tears, that they so desperately wanted to be rid of these kinds of anxieties.

If this is your struggle, you might deal with an extra dose of self-loathing and frustration about it. You might feel that it's understandable to break down in tears about a job loss, but you're embarrassed when you come to tears over hours lost deciding things like which flight to purchase. Or you might forgive yourself for agonizing about whether to ask someone out for a date, but you get angry at yourself when you're stuck in the greeting card aisle for twenty minutes, unsure of which birthday card to buy.

This kind of struggle doesn't usually end up on your radar as worth spending time addressing until it gets really bad, until you lose a much more significant amount of time and peace of mind. So we'll interface more with OCD experiences in this chapter, though this kind of severe anxiety can certainly attach itself to the big decision too. Also, this struggle does not have to cross the line into the definition of OCD in order to still be a significant headache.

The key principles we've covered in previous chapters will also apply for extreme anxieties over small decisions.

Learning to tolerate uncertainty and ambiguity is an act of faith, a step of trust in God's goodness in the midst of fear. Moving through what is terrifying is a step of great faith, precious in the eyes of God. And this is exactly what we're seeking to do. I want you to consider decisions about the small stuff as small steps of faith and trust. How we navigate decisions is part of our spiritual lives because it is part of our calling as God's stewards. But rather than waiting and listening deeply for whether God might want us to make one small decision or another, we will follow God best by regularly taking small risks—little acts of faith and trust—and stepping out and taking action in the world where he's called us. Making decisions requires living in an uncertain world, so this requires an ongoing life of humble trust and courageous effort.

DECISION-MAKING IS A SKILL

Making decisions requires acts of faith, so it is more than a life skill but a skill nonetheless—a process that requires practice. Effective practice, as with sports and music, means giving time to make conscious adjustments. In high school, after playing basketball less often, I noticed I was missing more shots than I used to. I had a problem in my shooting form; shots didn't have the arc they should. I had less confidence, more frustration, and I didn't even enjoy playing as much. But I knew that shooting a basketball wasn't just chance; it was a skill that could be developed. All kinds of adjustments could be made in order for me to see improvement. It's the same with anxiety. When anxiety attacks decisions about small purchases or plans, it's a chance to develop the skill, to make small adjustments so that you manage life a little better over time. You take one shot at a time. You still often miss, but you come to enjoy the game.

As stewards of God's creation, we naturally get a lot of joy when we see ourselves develop a skill, whether in sports, music, or our vegetable garden. It's the same with decisions. Over time, you experience peace and satisfaction in relaxing and ordering something a little risky off the menu, deciding to take an afternoon off, or making a small impulse purchase of flowers or a T-shirt just because it brought joy to you or someone else. Managing resources— time, money, work, and purchases—has as its ultimate goal loving God and others, which necessarily entails that you also seek to sustain these resources (including your body and soul!) through wise rhythms. Managing the resources doesn't mean spending them all at once or hoarding them all.[2] It means spending them according to orienting goals and values. We want our stewardship to come from a heart that is in line with God's heart. We'll never do this perfectly—it's not all in our control, and we often make decisions based on selfish desires or fear of others' opinions. But wisely managing life is a skill, which means it can be learned and developed. We grow in skills by practicing. And this requires (1) taking the risk, (2) accepting our imperfection, and (3) making incremental progress.

Skill Requires Risk

We've discussed the larger risks of big decisions in the previous two chapters, but small decisions carry risk too. Even if we go through a wise decision-making process, we know the outcome is uncertain. Our small decisions sometimes don't turn out well, and we may regret what we ordered at dinner or how we've planned a weekend. But this is part of how decisions involve learning and skill. We don't order the same thing off the menu if we don't like it. We avoid booking several social events in one

Saturday after we try it and feel too worn out at the end. We learn as we go, but it's not case law; it isn't something to keep track of or give much thought to for most small decisions. We're generally making progress with decision anxiety for small purchases and everyday plans when we become more convinced that it's not going to help to over-think it, ruminate, or second-guess ourselves. We entrust our small decisions to the Lord and generally want to give only small further amounts of time to them, resting in him and accepting both expected and unexpected outcomes.

We find this kind of rest and trust when we've come to a vital perspective change. This is the general accep-tance that we're always at risk of making mistakes and this is unavoidable. Our efforts to keep ourselves from risk will fail. Some of our decisions will be mediocre or bad, and some will seem good at the time but have seri-ous consequences. If we face this, our anxiety will spike. We'll feel a sense of panic or even terror. But if we stay with these feelings and do not try to argue them away, we will eventually start to despair of our efforts to avoid danger and suffering. And we will have the opportunity to entrust our decisions and our whole lives entirely to God to be kept safe there through the coming hardships. We can even start to feel something like rest in this act of trust.

This sense of restfulness and trust is easier said than done. Here is why: anxiety tends to read in dangers where there is ambiguity, and it nudges us to overfocus on risks.[3] So we feel a sense of panic, and we scramble to get to safety. And the only safety we can imagine is perfection. It doesn't feel safe to fail; it doesn't feel safe to be imper-fect. One risk that is difficult to grapple with is our own imperfection, so we'll look at this in more detail.

Skill Requires Accepting Imperfection

Practice does not make perfect, but it does help us get better at things. That's true with learning to play the piano, and it's also true with decisions. We risk errors and failures along the way. We're freer to make decisions when we accept the reality that our decisions are imperfect, and that we'll look back on some of today's decisions with regret. For example, had I known that my car was on empty, I'd have walked out of the house five to ten minutes earlier, rather than at the last minute. Had I known that this bag of chips was torn open, I wouldn't have bought it ten miles back on the road trip. With more knowledge, I'd have decided differently. But living with imperfect decisions makes it possible to make decisions at all.

We want to remove each individual decision from the perfectionistic pass or fail mindset. We have to fight this on at least two different fronts. First, we fight the ideas. We want to break down the whole system of beliefs and values that gives life to this anxiety. The Christian calling is to bear the name of Christ, to live oriented toward the faithfulness he calls us to, and not another name and reputation that seems to give safety. We might find a sense of refuge or a safe place to hide in academic performance or workaholism, but these ultimately won't hold us secure. It actually increases our insecurities because our performance is never truly perfect enough to support all this weight. We want to build our house upon a rock. This is an area for confession: "Lord, forgive me for turning to any refuge other than you."

Second, we fight the habits. Often we can get to the right ideas without them yet being worked out in our lives. So we want to take action steps that reject the habits of the perfectionistic way of life. Anxiety thrives when we treat decisions like tests that are graded as pass or fail, with no number grade in between. Anxious thoughts can intrude to raise a flaw, an uncertainty, or a possible negative outcome in a decision. So most options still feel like failure, and you're never confident you've passed the test. But remember, practice is not game day; the study guide is not the test.

All skills, including decision-making, require accepting imperfection and human limitation, not feeling too threatened by it but paying attention to it in how we practice. We wouldn't practice piano or basketball if we thought we were perfect; we couldn't practice if we felt we had to be perfect. We do our best practice when we relax, try, make small adjustments, and try again.

The Christian life is similar. We are in a process of discipleship and formation that requires practice (1 Timothy 4:7–8). We are imperfect, and God is completing the work he started in us, but that work is ongoing. Anxiety fixates on this imperfection, amplifying its dangers like a megaphone in our ears. Anxiety accuses us of foolishness, carelessness, arrogance, or selfishness. And how can you ever be sure some element of that isn't there—can you be fully sure that courage is not foolish, efficiency is not careless, confidence is not pride, or desire is not selfish?

We can be sure that imperfection is there. I once knew a pastor who said that if he had to be sure he was rid of every ounce of pride or sin before he got into the pulpit to preach, he could never preach. In one sense he took a risk every time he preached—*What if I'm just doing this because I like the sound of my own voice, or I feel important when people listen to me?* In another sense he stepped out in faith and trust, knowing that he was a sinner, that he needed Jesus just like the people he'd be speaking to, and that he was there to serve, even in his imperfection.

He might grade himself as a B+ that particular morning and feel his work is mediocre even when he has put in the hard work of preparation. But the paper is turned in; the opportunity has passed. He did not have to argue with himself to be certain he had not failed. He was oriented toward faithfulness, not perfection.

We're free to rest and walk in faithfulness when we know what grace is. Christians believe that Jesus died to cover and pay for our sins, and that God accepts and loves us as beloved children just as he accepts and loves his Son, Jesus. We believe God loves it when his children show love to their neighbors and even enemies, but he loves us even when our love falls short. Anxiety tells us the opposite: *God may love us, but he doesn't like us; God will not be understanding and generous toward our weakness and imperfection; God will leave us to our own bad decisions.* But the Bible speaks of God as a good Father who knows his children are weak (Psalm 103:14), who is patient with us, who is there to catch us when we fall. He will overcome evil with good and promises to turn even *evil* on its head, to take even the things intended for evil and subvert them in such a way as to bring good in the end—including our own bad decisions (Genesis 50:20; Romans 8:28).

When our anxieties tend to sound like accusations of moral failure, this message of grace is especially important. This is why Richard Baxter, the English pastor from the 1600s, said that Christians who live under a sense of constant accusation and anxiety must search out for themselves a pastor who "is rather judicious in his preaching and praying than passionate, except when he urgeth the gospel doctrines of consolation, and then the more fervently, the better."[4] We need to hear grace strong and clear. As anxious people, we worry that we are an exception, that grace is there for others but not us. So we desperately need to experience the grace and goodness of God. And we see this when we know him as the gentle shepherd, leading us one step at a time.

Skill Requires Incremental Progress

If decision-making is a skill, something we learn in our discipleship and Christian formation, then this means that God is doing things in us through the growing pains. The soreness after heavy lifting in this area is not muscle injury but muscle building. We are not being harmed when we accept the discomfort of taking risks and entrusting the results to God.

The best way to tackle the problem of decision anxiety in this area is to engage in a gradual process of facing your fears. I like to use Psalm 139 as a starting point in turning the anxious question of "what if" into the entrusting posture of "even if." As the psalm says,

> If I say, "Surely the darkness will hide me
>   and the light become night around me,"
> even the darkness will not be dark to you;
>   the night will shine like the day,
>   for darkness is as light to you. (Psalm 139:11b–12)

What if the darkness overtakes me? What if all is lost? Lord, even if I am in darkness, the darkness is as light to you—you'll reach me even there.

The process is direct but difficult. You step forward, *even if*. The goal is to entrust yourself to God, seek him as a refuge, and on purpose incrementally do the things that you are afraid of. The process goes best if other people are engaged in it with you, praying for you, encouraging you, and being present with you when you try to do scary things. Brief aside: do your best not to seek assurance from them or check with them too often. You'll make progress faster the more you're intentionally accepting the fact that you really can't have perfect assurance that you are making good decisions that will have good outcomes. Living a life of trusting God and faithfully engaging your calling through uncertainty is the priority here.

The process of facing your fears can start small. Here is a basic plan: Make a list of five to ten common small decisions that tend to get you stuck. Then assign each one a severity level, 1–10, with 1 being something that causes little distress and life disruption and 10 being one that paralyzes or terrifies you. Focus on the ones that cause the least distress first, and try to find ways to do exactly the thing you are afraid of. This basic outline is drawn from a method called Exposure and Response Prevention (ERP), but its core elements are things Christians have known for a long time: we grow through facing our fears and doing the hard thing, led by wise guides who care for us and alongside supportive friends who walk with us.

Here is an example: I've known teachers with significant anxiety about whether they are grading papers fairly. Grading is a useful illustration because it involves several small decisions throughout the various components of the project, then slightly larger decisions when looking at the whole project, and then the curve for the whole class. They know they aren't practicing favoritism, and they know they can tell the general difference between categories of good or bad projects. But they ask themselves whether they have been truly fair. They understand that other teachers may grade more quickly and less carefully, and they don't assume bad things about them. But they treat themselves as an exception to the rule, as though they are particularly in danger of an unfairness or inconsistency that will then have consequences on students' grades and careers. Let's say that grading all the papers and going back through again to review them once (rather than multiple times) causes distress at about a level 3/10, and grading a single time without checking is an 8/10.

Now imagine yourself as one of these teachers who struggles with decision anxiety. How could you grow in this area? The first step is to make sure to limit yourself to a single review of the projects at the end, paying attention to how much anxiety only performing a single review causes. As the anxiety increases, don't try to force it away. Your body is setting off an alarm because it perceives a threat, but don't let yourself try to lower the volume of the alarm—avoid doing the things you usually do to feel less anxious. Try your best not to ruminate, second-guess, or revisit justifications for why it is okay. Sit with the feeling that you might be in danger of unfairness, with the awareness that you can't perfectly guarantee that you are not being unfair. Watch the anxiety rise and gradually peak, then watch it recede. Feel free to breathe, take a walk, or pray conversationally.

Regarding prayer, make sure not to confess the "sin" of how you're grading, and avoid repetitive phrases in prayer or "just in case this is wrong" prayers. Anxious prayers often skew toward being less relational. But being close to God and others, being relationally connected, keeps us feeling more tethered and less anxious. It fosters the feeling that we're not alone, that God, our friends, and our families all love us, and that we can trust them to be with us as we endure what is really hard.

When practicing the method of grading (that originally caused level 3/10 anxiety) is causing even less anxiety, then you work up to the item with the next difficulty level, which perhaps would be limiting grading each paper to a certain number of minutes (this may cause level-5 anxiety), and then moving on, keeping the review at the end. The point is to gradually work up in the difficulty levels, enduring the distress faithfully and actively entrusting the results to God.

The process of facing our fears is a work of growing in perseverance. It's not pleasant, but staying with it will typically lead to progress. If you experience more severe disruption of life from these anxieties, you will likely want to consider finding a counselor with experience in anxiety and OCD.

Much of this basic plan will apply for anxiety that isn't quite as severe as OCD or scrupulosity. Struggling to order food or make purchases can be helped by adding time limits for deciding, sticking with the decision, and trying not to give voice to second-guessing and ruminating in regret. Purposefully taking the risk of a suboptimal or poor purchase in a reasonably short time frame will be uncomfortable, but tolerating this discomfort as a way to be freer to engage life or serve others will be worth the effort.

PRACTICAL HELPS FOR DECISION ANXIETY

Several practical things will be helpful to you as you engage in these efforts, especially if your anxieties are more severe. For centuries Christian writers have noticed that believers who struggled with ruminating in anxiety, and those with sensitive consciences, needed to spend less time in private, individual prayer. Lots of mental space doesn't seem to help a problem that thrives on ruminating. So prioritize praying aloud and with others for this season, and when you do pray by yourself, it's okay to simply pray through a hymn or psalm. It's okay to use these guardrails to avoid letting your prayer time further feed your anxiety.

Also look for "godly distraction," as I sometimes call it. Find good things to occupy yourself with, whether a novel, a good TV series, or gardening, especially focusing on filling the times when you are prone to ruminate.[5] Give yourself, in the right way, to the work at hand. Martin Luther said the first thing he would do when thoughts plagued him was to get out and do some work with his pigs.[6]

Other helps might come as a surprise to you. For example, the more you find ways to be engaged in serving people, the better. Look for opportunities to meet new people, and try to spend time with others who are grieving and seek to be a comfort to them.[7] Consider who God has placed within your sphere of influence or care, and seek to find ways to be of practical service to them or just give them a listening ear. One final piece of ancient advice from believers long ago who were quite familiar with the overscrupulous conscience is this: whatever anxiety tells you to do, do the opposite. If it tells you not to risk going out, go out. If it tells you to pray longer, don't. Consider anxiety an unreliable guide. Or to use another analogy, don't allow yourself to get into the boxing ring at all. If you get into trading punches and trying to argue it away, you'll usually lose. So don't give it any space, if you can help it at all. Putting these principles into action is not easy, but every bit of effort will be worth it in seizing back time and avoiding unnecessary anguish.

CONCLUSION

Decision-making is a skill, but actually it is a whole set of skills. It involves knowing our orienting values, knowing our situation, and knowing the options and possible

outcomes. It also involves knowing how to deliberate efficiently when values are in conflict or when the situation
could reasonably call for multiple good courses of action.
It also involves a holy boldness, a willingness to take good
risks and accept imperfection, entrusting our whole lives
to the Lord. This is all part of what we look for in Christian maturity and character over time.

To revisit the comparison to basketball, unfortu-
nately you have to miss a lot of shots to get better. You'll
have to make some mediocre decisions if you want to get
good and efficient at making small decisions. This is what
practice is like. And it's also not ultimately too different
from game day. In professional basketball games, the best
players still miss more than half of their shots. So it is with
our decisions. We are oriented toward faithfulness, not
toward perfect outcomes because those really aren't in our
control anyway.

But God does want us in the game. He wants us to
take shots. In the epistle of James, the condemnation is
not in their decision to take business trips and "buy and
sell, and get gain" (James 4:13 KJV) but in doing so arro-
gantly, as though the future is ours or we have control over
tomorrow. The call is to entrust all our actions and plans
to God, with a heart of, "if it is the Lord's will, we will live
and do this or that" (James 4:15). The future is not ours to
nail down. We are wholly dependent for today and tomorrow and through the troubles of each (Matthew 6:25–34).
We take the responsible actions of counting the cost when
we make decisions (Luke 14:25–33), but we want to keep
right at the front of our minds that all we have and all we
are does not belong to us but to God and we are simply
stewards. We work hard not to get lost and stuck in anxious indecisiveness because we don't want to lose sight of

the broader, holistic call of stewardship. We want to be free to serve the Lord, and anxiety leaves us bound. So I invite you to step out. The way forward is to accept discomfort incrementally, leaning into the risk of making a bad decision and entrusting the outcomes to God. And we even take a moment to rest because he holds all things.

QUESTIONS FOR REFLECTION

1. How much time and mental space are you losing to anxiety over small decisions? Is it creating complications in your relationships or ability to get things done?

2. What next steps can you take to start incrementally pushing back against the anxiety?

3. Read Psalm 139 and practice changing your own "what if" questions into "even if" statements in prayer.

CONCLUSION

"God's call gives a task that is more than a role, for it engages a man's whole person in the service of his Lord. That call is to being as well as doing, to status as well as service." — Ed Clowney[1]

In chapter 6 we reflected on the advice of one of the church fathers, Gregory the Great, who was concerned for people who struggled with decisions. He spoke of people who struggled to be decisive—the *fickle*—and also people who were overly decisive—the *obstinate*. The fickle person has trouble making decisions, knowing and articulating preferences, and exercising resolve. Gregory believed that a key problem for fickle people is they don't know who they are. Gregory understood, too, that problems with decisiveness (whether excess or deficiency) are not only socially inconvenient. As vices, he says, they are root problems that cause other problems.[2] And the risks are real. Fear brings all kinds of snares (Proverbs 29:25). Fear can silence us where we should speak and freeze us where we should act. Fear makes our lives small. It leads us to shrink back, anxiously looking externally for cues for a way to get to safety and studying risks. We sometimes lean on others for a strength we don't personally feel in our relationship with the Lord. Some of this is the natural mode of being younger in the faith and looking to the more mature to guide us. But growing up in Christ and in the body of Christ means you don't stay as a listener and learner only. You find your voice, and you start to speak the truth in love (Ephesians 4:15). You take your place as a gifted, called, and actively serving member of the body of Christ. You make decisions. And to do this, you need to know who you are, how God has gifted you, and how he has equipped and called you to engage your world. Gregory saw this appropriate confidence about who we are in Christ as the antidote to indecisiveness.

Becoming appropriately decisive does not swing the pendulum. You might be worried that if you risk making decisions with the right kind of firmness that you'll go too far and be stubborn, arrogant, or willful (or in Gregory's words, *obstinate*). Yes, it's a risk. But it's a risk worth living with because the goal is, of course, not arrogant decisiveness. We are aiming at being able to speak and act out of the confidence that comes from life in Christ. And, typically, fearful people are so much in danger of falling off one side of the wagon (indecisiveness) that they are not actually in danger of falling off the other (arrogance).

One of the benefits of the virtue framework that Gregory utilizes is to see both what is good and what is hard about different personal tendencies—and that often our greatest strengths and greatest weaknesses are connected. We have focused on the true problems associated with decision anxiety—and not only as a life complication but an area where spiritual growth and trust in the Lord are needed. But as you push back against decision anxiety, you may notice that it is, like most struggles, a fallen, broken, or skewed good thing. It is basically a good thing to be cautious, and often people who are not rash and too decisive can be a warm and welcoming presence for others. We can keep our personality strengths, seeing them as part of our gifting, while at the same time we push against its weaknesses.

Here is the goal: we aim to follow Christ with a humble confidence that leads to neither a deficit nor an excess of decisiveness. If we are rooted and grounded, we'll be able to say no when we need to, and our yes will be meaningful and not only conflict avoidance. We'll step out to love and serve neighbors. We'll follow God's calling and God's will in our lives. And with these roots, we'll be steady.

Being tossed by every wind is the opposite of being the blessed, fruitful tree (Psalm 1). But growing roots is difficult. It takes a while, and roots sometimes have to reach far into the dark to find water. Becoming rooted as a Christian is similarly difficult. Sometimes young, immature trees need to be fastened in place so that they can keep standing and grow stronger. Likewise, if you feel weak and easily tossed around, I want to invite you to see the Lord as securing the tree, fastening you to keep you rooted and stable, with his Word, his people, and his presence. As the song says, he will hold you fast:

> I could never keep my hold
> Through life's fearful path . . .
> He must hold me fast[3]

This is what decision anxiety ultimately longs for—a way through the fearful path, a place to keep our hold when everything feels vulnerable and precarious. And this is a Christian way to push back on the anxious thoughts: no, it is not the strength of our hold on Jesus that will keep our heads above the water, but the firmness of his hold on us.

With a steady, mature faith, there is freedom to decide, to be strong with our yes and no. Our decisions are less driven by our fear of people's responses. Instead, we're driven by a reverent fear of the Lord, which is the beginning of wisdom (Proverbs 9:10). The more wisely we steward what God has given us to manage, our time or efforts, the more we consciously give of ourselves to others, and so the more cheerfully we give. We know more who we are, and who we belong to, and so we know our role. Our decisions are increasingly motivated by a generous love. It is not compulsory giving but thoughtful service applied wisely to the need of the moment (2 Corinthians 9:6–7). Although we are part of the creation and therefore finite and limited, we serve a Creator with unlimited resources. So over time we find ourselves eager to serve and even eager to make decisions in service of God and his people. This kind of generous life operates from a mindset of abundance. "He who did not spare his own Son, but gave him up for us all—how will he not also, along with him, graciously give us all things?" (Romans 8:32). And what a beautiful life this makes.

With increasingly less crippling decision anxiety, we're freer to enjoy some of the sweetness of the Christian vision of God's salvation, a better security and goodness than we could ever get for ourselves. We experience the commitment of God "to rescue us from the hand of our enemies, and to enable us to serve him without fear in holiness and righteousness before him all our days" (Luke 1:74–75).

QUESTIONS FOR REFLECTION

1. Sometimes we keep anxiety around because it feels like it has an upside or silver lining. What are some of the parts of decision anxiety or overcautiousness that you have difficulty seeing as unhelpful and are harder to want to let go of? What are ways you deal with risk that need to be redeemed? What do you think this redemption might look like?

2. Think of one or two people with whom you can share what you have learned from this study, and ask them to pray for you to take some of the steps you've reflected on toward spiritual maturity.

3. Slowly and reflectively pray, "Heavenly Father, in you we live and move and have our being: We humbly pray you so to guide and govern us by your Holy Spirit, that in all the cares and occupations of our life we may not forget you, but may remember that we are ever walking in your sight; through Jesus Christ our Lord. Amen."[4]

ACKNOWLEDGMENTS

Thank you to the team at New Growth for the invitation to contribute to the Ask the Counselor series, for helpful and enjoyable conversations with Barbara and Rush, and for wise editorial help from Sarah and Ruth. I appreciate, too, that the Christian Counseling and Educational Foundation (CCEF) provided the opportunity to study and present on this topic for its 2019 National Conference. That seminar, "Decision Anxiety and the Peace of God," provided the occasion to work out many of the ideas now included in this book.

I am grateful as well for the board and my colleagues at Blue Ridge Christian Counseling, for the affirmation and encouragement for both my local day-to-day work and for outside opportunities such as this project.

What I've drawn from counseling for this project is not unique to any one person's story, but I owe thanks to the faithful Christians whom I've walked with in counseling over the years through their seasons of decision anxiety. They've taught me much about faith that thrives even through tough questions.

Dear friends and family have walked with me through my own share of anxieties about decisions. Joel, Eamon, and Dave are long-haulers. My parents have consistently modeled a mature and steady faith and invited me to it as well in many conversations about life decisions. My kids—Adriano, Shane, and Malia—have taught me a lot about fear and childlike faith. My wife Kelly's mature and steady faith has influenced me, for a decade now, and thoroughly influences anything I write. She also gave several evenings to offer edits and helpful input for this book—over and above!

ENDNOTES

Introduction

1. Emily P. Freeman, *The Next Right Thing: A Simple, Soulful Practice for Making Life Decisions* (Grand Rapids, MI: Revell, 2019), and her podcast with the same name.

2. Many of the stewardship themes I mention are drawn from the work of Old Testament scholar Doug Green. See Douglas J. Green, "Psalm 8: What Is Israel's King That You Remember Him?" (revised version of chapel address, Westminster Theological Seminary, Philadelphia, March 2, 2001, and the Reformed College of Ministries, Brisbane, September 5, 2002), https://www.academia.edu/7222228/Psalm_8_What_Is_Israels_King_That_You_Remember_Him.

3. Steven Johnson, *Farsighted: How We Make the Decisions That Matter Most* (New York: Riverhead Books, 2018).

4. J. I. Packer, *Finding God's Will* (Downers Grove, IL: InterVarsity Press, 1985).

5. Packer, 18–21.

6. B. Janet Hibbs and Anthony Rostain, *The Stressed Years of Their Lives: Helping Your Kid Survive and Thrive During Their College Years* (New York: St Martin's Press, 2019).

7. Greg Jao et al., "Relating to Others—Understanding Yourself," *Following Jesus without Dishonoring Your Parents* (Downers Grove, IL: InterVarsity, 1998), 72.

8. Sheila Wise Rowe, *Healing Racial Trauma: The Road to Resilience* (Downers Grove, IL: InterVarsity, 2020), 167.

9. Orlando Crespo, *Being Latino in Christ: Finding Wholeness in Your Ethnic Identity* (Downers Grove, IL: InterVarsity, 2003), 124–40.

10. Robert Chao Romero, *Brown Church: Five Centuries of Latina/o Social Justice, Theology, and Identity* (Downers Grove, Il: InterVarsity Academic, 2020).

Chapter 2

1. Rebecca Konyndyk DeYoung, "Resistance to the Demands of Love," in Christian Reflection series: Acedia (Waco, TX: The Center for Christian Ethics, 2013), 16; https://www.baylor.edu/content/services/document.php/212248.pdf.

2. Jeffrey Hughes, quoted in Kate Horowitz, "Why Making Decisions Stresses Some People Out," Mental Floss, February 27, 2017, https://www.mentalfloss.com/article/92651/why-making-decisions-stresses-some-people-out.

3. James K. A. Smith, *You Are What You Love: The Spiritual Power of Habit* (Grand Rapids, MI: Brazos, 2016), 3.

4. Robert C. Roberts, *Spiritual Emotions: A Psychology of Christian Virtues* (Grand Rapids, MI: Eerdmans, 2007).

5. "Teaching Note on Josef Pieper's *Leisure the Basis of Culture: An Integration of the Contemplative and Active Life*," University of St. Thomas (2010), https://www.stthomas.edu/media/catholicstudies/center/ryan/curriculumdevelopment/theologicalethics/Naughton-TeachingNote.pdf.

6. DeYoung, "Resistance to the Demands of Love."

Chapter 3

1. Angie Ward, "Michael Lindsay: Our Lives Are Full of 'Hinge Moments.' Here's How We Can Pray and Prepare," interview, *Christianity Today*, April 20, 2021, https://www.christianitytoday.com/ct/2021/may-june/michael-lindsay-hinge-moments-pray-prepare-decide.html.

2. *The Westminster Confession of Faith*, 3rd ed. (Lawrenceville, GA: Committee for Christian Education and Publications, 1990), 5.3)

3. See Vern S. Poythress, "Modern Spiritual Gifts as Analogous to Apostolic Gifts: Affirming Extraordinary Works of the Spirit within Cessationist Theology," *Journal of the Evangelical Theological Society* 39:1 (1996): 71–101.

4. J. I. Packer, *Finding God's Will* (Downers Grove, IL: Inter Varsity Press, 1985), 16–17.

5. Herman Bavinck, *Reformed Dogmatics: Holy Spirit, Church, and New Creation*, vol. 4 (Grand Rapids, MI: Baker Academic, 2008), 4:443ff.

6. Michael Gembola, "The Long Way Home: Counseling after Infidelity," CCEF National Conference, 2017, https://www.ccef.org/shop/product/long-way-home-counseling-infidelity/; and *After an Affair: Pursuing Restoration* (Phillipsburg, NJ: P&R, 2018).

7. Esther Perel, "Why Happy People Cheat: A Good Marriage Is No Guarantee Against Infidelity," *The Atlantic*, October 2017, https://www.theatlantic.com/magazine/archive/2017/10/why-happy-people-cheat/537882/.

Chapter 4

1. Quoted in Julia Beck, "When Are You Really an Adult?" *The Atlantic*, January 5, 2016, https://www.theatlantic.com/health/archive/2016/01/when-are-you-really-an-adult/422487/.

2. "Studies Show Normal Children Today Report More Anxiety than Child Psychiatric Patients in the 1950's," American Psychological Association, 2000, https://www.apa.org/news/press/releases/2000/12/anxiety; and Jean M. Twenge, "The Age of Anxiety? Birth Cohort Change in Anxiety and Neuroticism, 1952–1993," *Journal of Personality and Social Psychology* 79:6 (2000), 1,007–21.

3. Mary Ellen Flannery, "The Epidemic of Anxiety Among Today's Students," NEA Today, March 2019, https://www.nea.org/advocating-for-change/new-from-nea/epidemic-anxiety-among-todays-students; and Amy Ellis Nutt, "Why kids and teens may face far more anxiety these days," *Washington Post*, May 10, 2018, https://www.washingtonpost.com/news/to-your-health/wp/2018/05/10/why-kids-and-teens-may-face-far-more-anxiety-these-days/.

4. Jack O. Balswick, Pamela Ebstyne King, and Kevin S. Reimer, *The Reciprocating Self: Human Development in Theological Perspective* (Downers Grove, IL: IVP Academic, 2005), 190.

5. Jena McGregor, "This Former Surgeon General Says There's a 'Loneliness Epidemic' and Work Is Partly to Blame," *Washington Post*, October 4, 2017, https://www.washingtonpost.com/news/on-leadership/wp/2017/10/04/this-former-surgeon-general-says-theres-a-loneliness-epidemic-and-work-is-partly-to-blame/.

6. "The Social Dilemma: Social Media and Your Mental Health," McLean Hospital. January 21, 2022, https://www.

mcleanhospital.org/essential/it-or-not-social-medias-affecting-your-mental-health.

7. Justin Whitmel Earley, *The Common Rule: Habits of Purpose for an Age of Distraction* (Downers Grove, IL: IVP Books, 2019).

Chapter 5

1. Diane Langberg, *Counseling Survivors of Sexual Abuse* (Wheaton, IL: Tyndale, 1997), 23–29.

Chapter 6

1. "Renegade," featuring Taylor Swift, track 5 on *How Long Do You Think It's Gonna Last?*, Jagjaguwar, August 27, 2021.

2. Steven R. Tracy, *Mending the Soul: Understanding and Healing Abuse* (Grand Rapids, MI: Zondervan, 2005), 213–16.

3. Gregory the Great, *The Book of Pastoral Rule* (Crestwood, NY: St Vladimir's Seminary Press, 2007), 134.

4. Gregory the Great, 134–35.

5. Michael Gembola, "Helping the Unassertive Find Their Voice," *Journal of Biblical Counseling* 33:1 (2019), 46–64.

6. Paul E. Miller, *A Praying Life: Connecting with God in a Distracting World* (Colorado Springs, CO: NavPress, 2009), 121–22.

7. Deepak Reju, "4 Reasons for Writing *She's Got the Wrong Guy: Why Smart Women Settle*," Biblical Counseling Coalition, October 20, 2017, https://biblicalcounselingcoalition.org/2017/10/20/4-reasons-for-writing-shes-got-the-wrong-guy-why-smart-women-settle/.

8. Gerald Hiestand and Jay Thomas, *Sex, Dating, and Relationships: A Fresh Approach* (Wheaton, IL: Crossway, 2012), 47.

9. Michael Gembola, "The Use and Misuse of the Bible's Teaching on Dating and Courtship," CCEF National Conference, 2018, https://www.ccef.org/shop/product/the-use-and-misuse-of-the-bibles-teaching-on-dating-and-courtship/.

Chapter 7

1. Edmund P. Clowney, *Called to the Ministry* (Phillipsburg, NJ: P&R, 1964), 14.

2. Frederick J. Gaiser, "What Luther *Didn't* Say about Vocation," *Word & World* 25:4 (Fall 2005), 361.

3. Shane Claiborne, *The Irresistible Revolution: Living as an Ordinary Radical* (Grand Rapids, MI: Zondervan, 2006), 140.

4. Timothy Keller and Katherine Leary Alsdorf, *Every Good Endeavor: Connecting Your Work to God's Work* (New York: Penguin Books, 2016).

5. Alex Williams, "Why Is It Hard to Make Friends Over 30?" New York Times, July 13, 2012, https://www.nytimes.com/2012/07/15/fashion/the-challenge-of-making-friends-as-an-adult.html.

6. Amy L. Sherman, *Kingdom Calling: Vocational Stewardship for the Common Good* (Downers Grove, IL: IVP Books, 2011), 127.

7. Adam L. Gustine, *Becoming a Just Church: Cultivating Communities of God's Shalom* (Downers Grove, IL: IVP Books, 2019), 28.

8. Henry Ford, *Ford Ideals: Being a Selection from "Mr. Ford's Page" in the Dearborn Independent* (Dearborn, MI: The Dearborn Publishing Company, 1922), 53.

9. Alan Noble, *You Are Not Your Own: Belonging to God in an Inhuman World* (Downers Grove, IL: InterVarsity Press, 2021), 15.

10. Al Tizon, *Whole & Reconciled: Gospel, Church, and Mission in a Fractured World* (Grand Rapids, MI: Baker, 2018), 104.

11. Gustine, *Becoming a Just Church*, 28.

12. Gustine, 31.

13. Quoted in Gustine, 31.

14. Gustine, 34.

Chapter 8

1. BJ Thompson (@bj116), Twitter, July 31, 2021, 12:25 p.m., https://mobile.twitter.com/bj116/status/1421507437526388737.

2. Sally Schwer Canning, "Out of Balance: Why I Hesitate to Practice and Teach 'Self Care,'" *Journal of Psychology and Christianity* 30:1 (2011), 72.

3. Catherine A. Hartley and Elizabeth A. Phelps, "Anxiety and Decision-Making," *Biological Psychiatry* 72:2 (2012), https://doi.org/10.1016/j.biopsych.2011.12.027.

4. Richard Baxter, "The Cure of Melancholy and Overmuch Sorrow, by Faith and Physic," *The Practical Works of Richard Baxter: with a Life of the Author and a Critical Examination of His Writings by William Orme*, vol. 17, (London: Mills, Jowett, and Mills, 1830), 275.

5. Baxter, 274–75.

6. Martin Luther, *The Table Talk or Familiar Discourse of Martin Luther*, translated by William Hazlitt (London: David Bogue, 1848), 275.

7. Baxter, 275–76.

Conclusion

1. Edmund P. Clowney, *Called to the Ministry* (Phillipsburg, NJ: P&R, 1964), 10.

2. Gregory the Great, *The Book of Pastoral Rule* (Crestwood, NY: St Vladimir's Seminary Press, 2007), 135.

3. Ada Habershon (1861–1918), vv. 1–2, public domain; Matthew Merker, v. 3, alternate words, new words, and music (Getty Music, 2013); quoted by Justin Taylor, "Hymn of the Day: He Will Hold Me Fast," The Gospel Coalition, March 25, 2020, https://www.thegospelcoalition.org/blogs/justin-taylor/hymn-of-the-day-he-will-hold-me-fast/.

4. "A Collect for Guidance," *Book of Common Prayer* (Huntington Beach, CA: Anglican Liturgy Press, 2019), 669.

RESOURCES FOR FURTHER READING

For learning with a format or template

- Kevin DeYoung offers a simple, three-step approach in *Just Do Something: A Liberating Approach to Finding God's Will* (Chicago, IL: Moody, 2009), 96.
- Garry Friesen and J. Robin Maxson summarize an approach they call the apostle Paul's in six steps in *Decision Making and the Will of God: A Biblical Alternative to the Traditional View* (Sisters, OR: Multnomah, 2004), 239.
- James C. Petty provides a thorough, seven-step process in *Step by Step: Divine Guidance for Ordinary Christians* (Phillipsburg, NJ: P & R Publishing, 1999), 193–261.

For understanding how God's will and Christian values can be brought to bear on our decision-making

- Emily P. Freeman writes what seems well postured for the decision challenges of midlife in *The Next Right Thing: A Simple, Soulful Practice for Making Life Decisions* (Grand Rapids, MI: Revell, 2019).
- Wayne Grudem gives a concise and readable engagement with the topics of God's will and decisions in *What the Bible Says about How to Know God's Will* (Wheaton, IL: Crossway, 2020).

- J. I. Packer gives a short, general understanding of God's will and a Christian's calling in *Finding God's Will* (Downers Grove, IL: InterVarsity Press, 1985).
- J. I. Packer offers his fuller thoughts on this theme in *God's Plans for You* (Wheaton, IL: Crossway, 2001).

For guidance related to decision-making and vocation

- D. Michael Lindsay, *Hinge Moments: Making the Most of Life's Transitions* (Downers Grove, IL: IVP, 2021).
- Erica Young Reitz, *After College: Navigating Transitions, Relationships and Faith* (Downers Grove, IL: IVP Books, 2016).
- Amy L. Sherman, *Agents of Flourishing: Pursuing Shalom in Every Corner of Society* (Downers Grove, IL: 2022).

For severe anxiety or OCD that afflicts your spiritual life and decisions

- Joseph Ciarrocchi, *The Doubting Disease: Help for Scrupulosity and Religious Compulsions* (Mahwah, NJ: Paulist Press, 1995).